Bookkeeping Made Simple

Louis W. Fields

Revised by **Richard R. Gallagher, D.B.A.**

Edited and prepared for publication by The Stonesong Press, Inc.

A MADE SIMPLE BOOK

DOUBLEDAY

NEW YORK LONDON TORONTO SYDNEY AUCKLAND

Edited and prepared for publication by The Stonesong Press
Managing Editor: Sheree Bykofsky
Editor: Lillian R. Rodberg
Design: Blackbirch Graphics, Inc.
Editorial Consultants: Lynne Luper, M.B.A., Toni Geller

Published by Doubleday, a division of
Bantam Doubleday Dell Publishing Group, Inc.
666 Fifth Avenue, New York, New York 10103

MADE SIMPLE and DOUBLEDAY are trademarks of Doubleday,
a division of Bantam Doubleday Dell Publishing
Group, Inc.

Library of Congress Cataloging-in-Publication Data

Fields, Louis W.
    Bookkeeping made simple.

    A MADE SIMPLE BOOK
    Includes index.
    1. Bookkeeping.   I. Gallagher, Richard R.
II. Title.
HF5635.F46   1989   657′.2   88–33616
ISBN 0–385–23882–7

CONTENTS

PART ONE

THE BASIC FUNCTIONS OF BOOKKEEPING

CHAPTER ONE

What Bookkeeping Is All About

TERMS YOU'LL NEED TO KNOW

accounts payable	*current liabilities*	*operating statement*
accounts receivable	*debit*	*owner's equity*
asset	*equity*	*plant assets*
balance sheet	*inventory*	*prepaid items*
bonds payable	*liability*	*short-term notes payable*
cash	*long-term liabilities*	*supplies*
credit	*long-term notes*	*transaction*
current assets	*mortgages payable*	*wages payable*

You may have heard that "the business of America is business." What is business? To define it formally, we might say that business consists of "all commercial activities designed to sell goods and services to customers at a profit." Less formally, though, any enterprise in which we receive, spend, borrow, save, and (possibly) lend money is a business, whether it is a teenager's paper route, a drugstore, a TV repair shop, a manufacturing plant—or even a family. A professional practice like a doctor's or a dentist's is also a business in the sense we are using here. Business is a game with many players, and bookkeepers keep the score.

In days gone by, business records were kept in big cloth-covered volumes: "the

> **Bookkeeping means keeping records of what is bought, sold, owed, and owned; what money comes in, what goes out, and what is left.**

books." Today, the people who keep the records are still called bookkeepers, even though they don't use quill pens and the "books" may be computer disks. Whether you will be keeping books with pen and paper or on a computer screen, the principles you will use stay the same. What bookkeeping is all about is telling the owner(s) of a business (who might be yourself) how much money has come into the business, how much has gone out, what is owned, what is owed, and whether the business is gaining or losing in value.

In this chapter you'll learn some basic terms and principles that you'll be using as long as you keep books. You'll be introduced to some bookkeeping "tools" that are more fully explained in later chapters. The physical form of these tools may change over time, but they are used for the same purposes by all businesses and are understood throughout the world of commerce. Essentially, bookkeepers use the same methods whether they are working for a sole proprietorship (owned by one person), a partnership, or a corporation. To keep things simple, we will describe bookkeeping operations in terms of a sole proprietorship. Chapter 15 contains a brief explanation of partnerships, and Chapter 16 discusses corporate bookkeeping.

Keeping a Record of Transactions

A **transaction** is any business dealing that involves money. It may be a sale, a purchase, a loan, a lease payment, or any activity in which money is shifted from one "place" (account) to another. The money may be in the form of cash (currency), check, or money order, or it may be in the form of a promise to pay such as a charge slip, a note, or a mortgage.

When your news carrier delivers a paper, that is a transaction. When the carrier pays the newspaper company, that is a transaction. When the carrier collects from you, it is a transaction. And when the carrier pays the newspaper company, the newspaper pays its reporters and suppliers, and the suppliers in turn pay their workers and suppliers, each of these instances (and the many others that accompany them) is a transaction.

Your first responsibility as a bookkeeper is to keep a record of every transaction that occurs in the business you work for. Unless you do this accurately, you cannot fulfill your responsibility of keeping score. Your basic tool for recording transactions is the *journal*, which is explained fully in Chapter 2. In the journal, you enter transactions in chronological order—that is,

> **Your first responsibility as a bookkeeper is to keep a record of all transactions, large and small.**

> ***Remember:*** **Every credit entry must be balanced by a debit entry.**

the order in which they occur. This is called making a *journal entry*. Later, the journal entries are transferred to a various number of records called *accounts* (this process is called *posting*) and used to prepare many kinds of financial reports.

A bookkeeping entry is either a **debit** or a **credit.** A debit is always entered in the left-hand column. A credit is always entered in the right-hand column. Although people often assume that a debit means a

subtraction and a credit means an addition, this is not necessarily the case. There are rules that determine whether something is a debit or a credit; these rules pertain in part to what is called the "normal account balance" account. Not all these rules will make sense to you, especially at first.

As you'll see, the basic principle behind double-entry bookkeeping, the kind you are learning, is that debits and credits must always balance (equal each other). This means that *an item that is credited in one place must be debited somewhere else.* Every transaction eventually involves both a credit and a debit. Whether to debit or credit an item often confuses beginning bookkeepers. Answering this question is what much of this book is about.

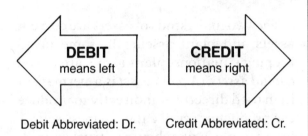

Debit Abbreviated: Dr.   Credit Abbreviated: Cr.

THE SECRET OF RITA'S LOCKED DRAWER

Rita had been keeping the books for fifty years. "She knows everything there is to know," the others told newcomers. "The boss depends on her." Rita was a creature of habit. Every morning she would pour herself a cup of tea. Then, before settling down to work, she would look over her shoulder to make sure no one was close by before opening the first left-hand drawer of her desk a few inches and peering inside. Then she would shut and lock it. One night, Rita died in her sleep. Her curious colleagues opened the locked drawer to clean it out. They found it empty except for a yellowed slip of paper pasted to the bottom. It read:

> CREDITS GO ON THE RIGHT; DEBITS GO ON THE LEFT

After your journal entries have been posted to various accounts, you will be able to prepare financial statements to summarize the condition of the business. Is it making a profit or operating at a loss? Are the owners increasing their investment, or is the business losing value? We will talk more about the meaning of these questions in later chapters. For now, you need to know the purpose of two kinds of financial statements, the balance sheet and the operating statement.

① The **balance sheet** shows what the business owns (assets), what it owes (liabilities), and what the owners would have left if the business paid everything it owes out of everything it owns (the **owners' equity,** sometimes called *capital* or *net worth*). The **operating statement** (sometimes called a *profit and loss statement* or *P&L*) lists income over a specified period such as a year or a calendar quarter, and subtracts expenses over the same period to show whether a profit was earned or a loss incurred.

Assets: What the Business Owns

Any property the business owns, and any claim it has on the property of others, is called an **asset.** Remember that you list any business property as an asset, regardless of whether it is fully paid for. Any amount owed on the property will be listed as a **liability** (see the next section).

Assets include such things as:
○ land
○ buildings
○ equipment
○ tools
○ cash
○ accounts receivable
○ inventories
○ materials

Any *thing* of value to the business is an asset. When an asset is acquired, you record it in the dollar amount paid for it, for example, "Ford delivery van, $23,500."

How Are Assets Classified?

The two main kinds of assets are current assets and plant assets. (In some bookkeeping situations, plant assets are called *capital assets.*) A *plant asset* is a permanent item used directly or indirectly to produce the product or service the business sells—for example, a warehouse, a truck, a milling machine, or a sales counter. Inventory (stock of goods to be sold) and materials (stock of raw materials or components) are current assets.

Current assets continually change. They are listed on the balance sheet in order of their *liquidity*, the speed with which they can be turned into cash. Cash (on hand or in a demand deposit in the bank) is therefore listed first. Cash is the first resource for paying bills. **Accounts receivable** is the money owed by customers of the business for goods or services they have purchased on credit. They are listed next because it is

---

Assets consist of anything the business owns and any claims it has against the property of others.

assumed they will soon become cash. Next are listed inventories (goods held for sale), supplies, and prepaid items such as insurance and rent paid in advance. In the list below, plant assets and current assets are listed and defined. Note the order in which they appear in standard bookkeeping practice.

Current Assets

Cash: The total of currency (dollars), coins, money orders, checks, bank drafts, and letters of credit the firm has on hand or in bank accounts from which the money can be drawn immediately (demand deposits).

Accounts Receivable: The amount owed by customers who purchased goods and services for which they have not yet paid.

Inventories: The dollar value in actual cost of goods a firm has for sale (that is, its stock).

Supplies: Materials used in conducting the daily operations of the business, such as stationery, computer disks, typewriter ribbons (office supplies) or lubricating oil, paint, solder (factory materials).

Prepaid Items: Amounts already paid for services the business has yet to receive—for example, insurance.

To summarize, current assets consist of (1) cash or items that will become cash in the foreseeable future because they are intended for sale (or for the manufacture of goods that will be sold), and (2) items that the business will consume within a year.

Plant Assets (Sometimes called capital assets):

Land: The value of acreage owned by the business at actual purchase price.

Buildings: Purchase price or construction cost of structures, including surveys, architects' fees, engineering fees, permits, etc.

Equipment: Itemized list of the price paid for machines, vehicles, boilers, conveyors, shelving, and durable tools, as well as office equipment, computers, typewriters, desks and other furniture. The value of equipment is subject to depreciation (see Chapter 10).

Note that whether an item is listed as a current asset or a plant asset depends on its intended purpose. If you had an appliance business, you would list air conditioners held for sale as current assets, but an air conditioner installed to keep the store cool would be a plant asset. The deciding factor in determining whether something is a plant asset is whether it will be retained for use *within the business* at some time.

Any item may be a current asset or a plant asset according to whether you plan to sell it or to use it in the business.

Equities: What the Business Owes Itself and Others

An **equity** is any debt a business owes, whether to outsiders or its owners. **Liabilities** are legal claims against the business by persons or corporations other than the owners. These claims come before the rights of the owners. They may consist of money owed to suppliers or vendors for inventory or supplies, to banks or loan companies for equipment, money owed for taxes, and so on. The amount that would be left after all debts of the business had been satisfied is the **owner's equity** (or *owners' equity* if the business has more than one owner).

Like assets, liabilities are classified as being short-term or long-term. *Current liabilities* are like current assets; *long-term liabilities* are like plant assets. Generally, liabilities are considered current if they must be a paid within the current accounting year. As you will see in Chapter 2, total assets and total liabilities and capital must balance—that is, equal each other.

Liabilities are listed in the following order:

Current Liabilities

Accounts Payable: Bills owed to creditors such as vendors or suppliers.

Wages Payable: Payroll due.

Short-Term Notes Payable: Borrowing that must be repaid within the current accounting year.

Long-Term Liabilities

Long-Term Notes Payable: Borrowing to be repaid after one year.

Mortgages Payable: Balance due on business mortgages.

Bonds Payable: Amounts due to bondholders (applies to corporations).

With these basic terms in mind, you are ready to address what is called the "accounting equation" and the basic functions of bookkeeping.

Liabilities are legal claims against the business held by others; they take precedence over owners' claims.

CHAPTER TWO

The Bookkeeping Equations: The Balance Sheet and the Operating Statement

---

TERMS YOU'LL NEED TO KNOW

balance sheet
balance sheet equation
capital
expenses

initial capital
net income
operating statement
revenues

The most basic principle of bookkeeping is that what is owned must always balance what is owed. This can be expressed as the **balance sheet equation.**

ASSETS = EQUITIES

ASSETS = LIABILITIES + CAPITAL
(Creditors' Equity)   (Owners' Equity)

The Accounting Equation

The fundamental accounting equation is often abbreviated to $A = L + C$. It means that assets must equal equities, which consist of liabilities (the creditors' equity) plus **capital,** the owners' equity in their business. (The economic system of the United States, capitalism, takes its name from the fact that the equity of U.S. business enterprises belongs to private individuals, singly or in voluntarily formed groups.)

To express in bookkeeping language how much you own of an automobile that cost $15,000 and on which you owe the bank $10,000, you would take the asset value ($15,000) and subtract the liability of $10,000 (a creditor's equity) to arrive at the capital, or owner's equity, of $5,000. Your balance sheet would then be:

$$\$15,000 = \$10,000 + \$5,000$$
$$(\text{asset}) = (\text{liability}) + (\text{capital})$$
$$A = L + C$$

An efficient bookkeeper will check frequently to verify that A does indeed equal L plus C. If it does not, an error has been made somewhere and the books are not in balance.

The Balance Sheet

When all the assets and liabilities have been totaled, they are summarized on a statement called a **balance sheet.** Assets are listed by categories on the left side and equities (liabilities and capital) on the right. The sum of the left side must equal, or balance, the sum on the right. **Figure 2.1** shows a typical balance sheet.

Among the assets of the business is the *initial capital* put into the business by its owner(s). For example, when you start a business, you may put some of your savings into the business checking account so that you can meet start-up expenses and

Richdale Company
Balance Sheet
Dec. 31, 19____

ASSETS			LIABILITIES		
CURRENT ASSETS			CURRENT LIABILITIES		
Cash	$15,000		Accounts Payable	$3,000	
Inventory	10,000		Note Payable	5,000	
Prepaid Insurance	5,000				
Total Current Assets		$30,000	Total Current Liabilities		$8,000
PLANT ASSETS			LONG-TERM LIABILITIES		
Truck	$10,000		Mortgage Payable	$25,000	
Machines	5,000		Total Long-Term Liabilities		$25,000
Total Plant Assets		$15,000	Total Liabilities		$33,000
			CAPITAL		
			Owner's Equity		$12,000
TOTAL ASSETS		$45,000	TOTAL LIABILITIES and CAPITAL		$45,000

Figure 2.1

Initial capital consists of the money and assets the owner(s) contribute to start a business.

---

keep the business going until money from customers begins to come in. Or you may put a truck or station wagon that belongs to you into the business name. These become part of the capital, also called the net worth, owners' equity, or proprietorship interest.

How would a bookkeeper handle such a transaction? Remember that $A = L + C$. Suppose you put up $20,000 in cash to start your business. The transaction would increase your cash on hand (an asset) by $20,000. But it would also increase your capital by $20,000. Thus:

$$A = L + C$$
$$\$20,000 \text{ cash} = \$0 + \$20,000 \text{ capital}$$

Next, suppose your business purchases $5,000 worth of plastic toys for resale. This transaction would be recorded as follows:

$$Assets = Liabilities + Capital$$
$$\$20,000 = \$0 \qquad + \$20,000$$
$$- 5,000 \text{ (for the cash spent)}$$
$$+ 5,000 \text{ (for the plastic toys bought)}$$
$$\$20,000 = \$0 \qquad + \$20,000$$

The purchase reduced your cash on hand (an asset) by $5,000, but it increased your inventory (also an asset) by $5,000. Both sides of the equation still balance.

To deliver your toys, you now purchase a truck costing $15,000. You put down $3,000 from your business cash account

and sign a note, or equipment loan, for $12,000. Now your account looks like this:

$$Assets \quad = \quad Liabilities \quad + Capital$$
$$\$20,000 \quad = \quad \$0 \qquad\qquad + \$20,000$$
$$- 5,000$$
$$+ 5,000$$
$$+ 15,000 \text{ (truck)}$$
$$- 3,000 \text{ (cash)} \quad \$12,000 \text{ (note)}$$
$$\$32,000 \quad = \quad \$12,000 \qquad + \$20,000$$

When you add all the columns, you find that one side still equals the other side.

Now suppose you sell $1,000 of the plastic toys for $1,333. This transaction reduces your inventory (assets) by $1,000 and increases your cash on hand (assets) by $1,333. Does this unbalance your accounts? No, because $333 of the amount received for the toys is profit; it is added to your capital (see **Figure 2.2**) Your accounts now read:

$$Assets = Liabilities + Capital$$
$$\$32,333 = \$12,000 \quad + \$20,333$$

Of course, these are very simplified examples, and the real transactions you will be working with as a bookkeeper are more complicated. For now, however, practice keeping your accounts in balance by continuing with your hypothetical toy business:

o You sell $500 more toys "on account"; that is, your customer has not yet paid for them.

The Balance Sheet Equation

Assets = Liabilities + Capital

(also called Owners' Equity)

Increase | Increase with | Increase with
with Debits | Credits | Credits

Revenues − Expenses = Net Income

Increase with | Increase with
Credits | Debits

Figure 2.2

○ You make a $1,000 payment on the truck loan.

Can you see how each of these transactions affects your $A = L + C$ equation? Have you kept the equation in balance?

The Net Income Formula

In addition to handling assets and liabilities, bookkeepers must work with revenues and expenses. **Revenues** are the earnings of the business, the money that comes in from the sale of products (*sales revenue*) or services (*service revenue*). You earn sales revenue by selling goods from inventory, and service revenues from selling time and talent. Many businesses earn both kinds of revenue; for example, a TV business earns sales revenue each time a television set or VCR is sold. It earns service revenues through repairs and perhaps through cassette rentals. Revenues are an inflow of assets, whether they are in the form of cash or in the form of accounts receivable.

Expenses are the costs of doing business; they constitute an outflow of assets. To use the TV store example again, sets purchased for resale, the rent for the store, the decorative displays, the sales slips, and the salary and commission of the sales people are all expenses. Expenses may flow out in the form of cash or by incurring accounts payable.

When expenses are subtracted from revenues, the sum remaining is **net income.** You might casually refer to this as profit, but profit takes a number of forms: gross profit, net profit, or profit before or after

Revenues represent an inflow of capital;
expenses represent an outflow of capital.

Net income is the "bottom line"—what is left after all expenses of the business have been met.

taxes. Net income is what is left after *all* expenses have been met; you'll hear it called "the bottom line" because that is where it appears on the accounting page. Expressed as a formula, the final calculation of net income looks like this:

$$R - E = NI$$
$$(\text{revenues}) - (\text{expenses}) = (\text{net income})$$

The Operating Statement

Revenue, expenses, and net income are summarized on a statement called an **operating statement.** Operating statements reveal all revenues earned and expenses incurred by a business during a specified time period: a month, a quarter (three months), six months, or a year. If yearly period used is from January 1 through December 31, it is called a *calendar year.* If some other 365-day period is used (for example, a year calculated from the date the business opened), it is called a *fiscal year.* "Fiscal" means financial.

Figure 2.3 shows a typical operating statement. Some people call this an income statement, a statement of income and expense, or even a profit and loss statement, but "operating statement" is the term most often used by professionals. Pay particular attention to the location of dollar signs, the location of the columns, and the single and double underscoring.

Dollar signs appear by the top number in every column and at every total. A column total shifts to the left when it is to be used in further addition or subtraction. Underscoring appears below every subtotal, and double underscoring appears beneath the final amount.

Keeping the records of income and expenses and translating them into operating statements and balance sheets are the basic functions of all bookkeeping, whether the business employs only its owner or a thousand workers in many locations.

Tom's TV Emporium
Operating Statement
for the Year Ended 12/31/19____

REVENUES		
Sales Revenue	$200,000	
Service Revenue	100,000	
Total Revenues		$300,000
EXPENSES		
Wages	$90,000	
Rent	80,000	
Insurance	70,000	
Taxes	20,000	
Advertising	5,000	
Telephone	1,000	
Total Expenses		$266,000
NET INCOME		$34,000

Figure 2.3

EXERCISES

2.1 Using the work sheet on the facing page, prepare a balance
sheet using the following information for the Jones Company
on June 30, 19___.

Cash	$ 600
Inventory	1,000
Prepaid rent	2,000
Store equipment	1,400
Typewriter	900
Accounts payable	300
60-day bank note	1,200
Accounts receivable	2,500
3-year bank note	6,000
Owner's equity	900

2.2 Identify each of the following as an asset, a liability, or capital.
1. cash
2. accounts payable
3. John Smith, capital
4. interest due to bank
5. supplies on hand
6. land and building
7. insurance paid in advance
8. account payable

2.3 Create an operating statement for Amy's Beauty Shoppe using the
following information: From January 1 through March 31 the owner
deposited $50,000 for cutting and blow-drying hair and $25,000 for
selling hair spray and conditioners. The rent for the quarter was
$6,000, electricity $1,000, wages $23,000, and insurance $900. Use
a separate sheet of accounting paper.

Check your answers against the Solutions at the end of the book.

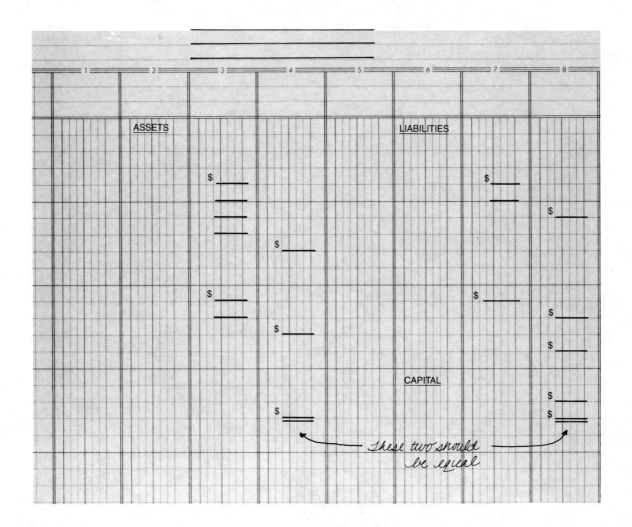

PART TWO

THE ACCOUNTING CYCLE

CHAPTER THREE

The Journal

TERMS YOU'LL NEED TO KNOW

accounting cycle

compound entries

double entry system

entry

journal

normal account balances

T account

The procedures you will be learning in Chapters 3 through 8 are stages in the **accounting cycle.** Picture the cycle as a circle that repeats itself again and again throughout the life of the business, just as the seasons repeat themselves each year.

The Accounting Cycle

The cycle starts when a transaction occurs. Every time a transaction is made, it must be recorded (a process called journalizing). Each transaction brings about a change in one or more accounts: assets, liabilities, capital, revenues, or expenses; these changes must be recorded also (posting). Your accounts must be verified for accuracy (trial balance). Once each business year, or more often as needed, you will prepare a worksheet so that you can summarize these changes in balance sheets and operating statements. You must make adjustments and enter for changes that are not supported by documents such as sales slips. Then, you will "close the books" in preparation for the beginning of the next cycle.

The Accounting Cycle

1. **TRANSACTION**
occurs

2. **JOURNALIZING**
Transactions are entered
in a journal

8. **CLOSING**
Books are prepared
for next cycle

3. **POSTING**
Journal entries are trans—
ferred to ledger accounts

7. **ADJUSTING JOURNAL ENTRIES**
Work sheet/ financial
statements are posted to ledger

6. **FINANCIAL STATEMENTS**
Balance sheet and operating
statement are prepared

4. **TRIAL BALANCE**
Accounts are verified
totaled, and balanced

5. **WORK SHEET**
Adjustments are made
to prepare for
financial statements

The Journal

The daily "diary" in which each transaction is recorded, or entered, is called the *general journal*, or simply the **journal.** In the journal, transactions are listed in chronological order—that is, in the order of their date of occurrence.

The journal is the starting place for all bookkeeping; for that reason it is called the *book of original entry.*

The Double Entry System

In keeping your journal, you work with written records or documents such as vendors' invoices, customers' sales slips, records of charges, shipping papers (bills of lading), bank deposit records, and so on. Each time you make such a record, you are making an **entry;** in the **double entry system,** each transaction is recorded twice, as a credit to one account and a debit to an-

---

The journal, or "book of original entry," is the starting place for all bookkeeping activities.

> **The major advantage of the double entry system of bookkeeping is that it provides a continual check on accuracy.**

other. In order for the "books" to be "in balance," the total of debits in all accounts must equal the total of credits in all accounts. If they do not, you know immediately that an error has been made: an entry was omitted, or made incorrectly. Thus the double entry system provides a continual check on accuracy.

Making Journal Entries

To begin your journal, you "head up" a two-column journal page or sheet with the name of the business and the words "General Journal." The left-hand column is headed "Dr." (the abbreviation for debit) and the right-hand column "Cr." (the abbreviation for credit). Since the column dividers resemble the letter "T," this arrangement is called a **T account**. On the far left is a column for the date. **Figure 3.1** shows a journal page prepared to accept entries.

Note that journal entries are not totaled. The data from these entries is totaled when a *trial balance* is taken, at which time the totals are transferred to the operating statement and the balance sheet (see Chapter 7).

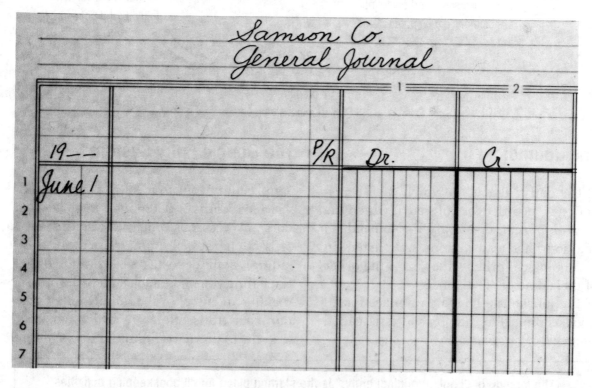

Figure 3.1

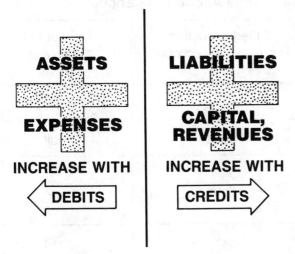

Figure 3.2

Debit or Credit?

Now you are ready to enter transactions. Before you can begin, though, you need to know whether a given transaction should be entered in the debit (Dr.) column or in the credit (Cr.) column. Every entry you make in the journal will eventually be entered ("posted") to a ledger account. Doing this is discussed in Chapter 4, but to make the journal entry, you need to know whether a debit or a credit increases or decreases the kind of account it applies to. Memorize these rules:

○ Assets *increase* with debits and *decrease* with credits.
○ Liabilities (creditors' equity) *increase* with credits and *decrease* with debits.
○ Capital (owners' equity) *increases* with credits and *decreases* with debits.
○ Revenues *increase* with credits and *decrease* with debits.
○ Expenses *increase* with debits and *decrease* with credits.

Keep **Figure 3.2** in front of you until you become perfectly acquainted with the rules for using debits and credits in making journal entries. Note that if the figure used minus signs (to signify decreases) each of the items would be listed on the opposite side.

Normal Account Balances

In any given account, increases will exceed decreases under normal circumstances. For example, a Cash account would normally have a positive total rather than a negative one. Increases to assets will ordinarily exceed decreases (unless the business is losing money). You can see that having a balance of −$80 in the cash account would be awkward. So would having a minus (credit) balance in the land or building accounts.

Table 3.1 shows the "normal account balance" for each category of account, as well as how to treat a transaction. Since revenues customarily grow, the normal balance in that account is a credit. Expenses also grow, so the normal balance is a debit. A balance that is out of normal circumstance may signal an error.

Now, review what you have learned by considering whether you would use a debit or a credit journal entry to show the following:

○ An increase in cash
○ A decrease in inventory
○ An increase in machinery
○ The spending of cash
○ Going into debt (increasing a liability)
○ Paying a bill that is due
○ Earning revenue from a sale
○ Increasing your (the owner's) capital

Table of Debits & Credits Showing Normal Account Balances

Category of Account	If the transaction increases the account enter a . . .	If the transaction decreases the account enter a . . .	The normal balance is a . . .
Asset	debit	credit	debit
Liability	credit	debit	credit
Capital (Owner's Equity)	credit	debit	credit
Revenue	credit	debit	credit
Expenses	debit	credit	debit

Table 3.1

Each time bookkeepers enter a transaction in the journal, they must go through the following thinking process:

1. What accounts are affected by this entry? (Note that more than one account is affected.)
2. Are these accounts assets, liabilities, capital, revenues, or expenses?
3. Does the transaction increase or decrease them?
4. Does this information call for a debit entry or a credit entry?

For example: The cash sales for this week were $12,000. You need to enter this transaction in the journal. To decide which accounts are affected, you use the following thought process: "I know that the event involves cash sales. I know cash is an asset and sales is a revenue. I see that cash (an asset) increased, and sales (a revenue) also increased. An increase in an asset calls for a debit, while an increase in a revenue calls for a credit." Your journal entry would look like **Figure 3.3.** You can get additional practice with Exercise 3.1 at the end of the chapter.

Compound Entries

Sometimes a transaction affects more than two accounts. For example, suppose your business purchased a $23,000 truck for $3,000 down and signed a note payable for $20,000. In this case two lines are used to record the two credits. The total of the credits should equal the total of the debits. This transaction is shown in **Figure 3.4.**

Journal Entries for Revenues and Expenses

Revenue such as the income from the sale of goods serves to add to the owners' capital account. For this reason, the revenue account is increased with credits.

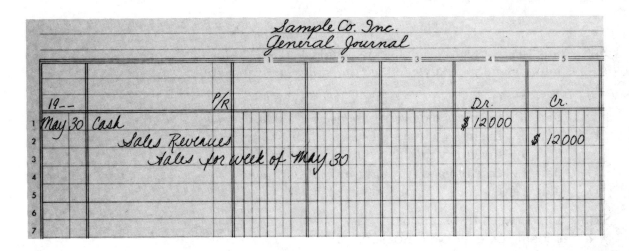

Figure 3.3

Conversely, expenses increase with debits and serve to reduce the owners' capital account.

A helpful guideline is to remember that expenses are almost always debited. The exception would occur in the case of an overpayment. When expenses are entered in the journal, the credit is usually to cash.

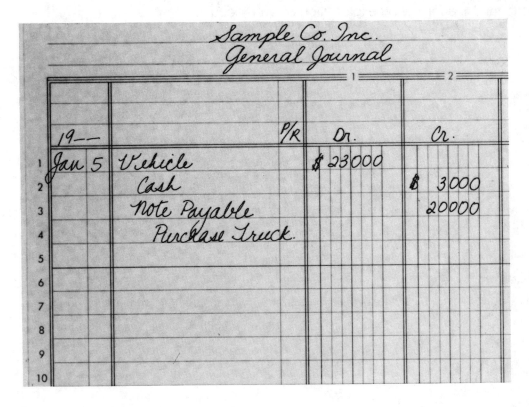

Figure 3.4

EXERCISES

3.1 Using the work sheet on page 31, head up a journal for the Young Company and journalize (enter) the following transactions:

     Jan. 2. Owner put $10,000 in cash into business.
     Jan. 3. Business paid rent expense of $1,000.
     Jan. 5. Business purchased supplies for $50 cash.
     Jan. 9. Inventory purchased for $900 on account.
     Jan. 14. Sale of goods brought in $250 revenue.
     Jan. 29. Owner took out $500 in cash.

Skip a line between transactions.
- Remember to date every transaction.
- Begin by writing the year only, once on each page, in the upper left.
- Write the month below, once on each page.
- Then write the day for every transaction as shown in the preceding illustrations.
- Do not write the year or month again unless it changes.
- The first entry will be a debit entry, followed by the credit entry, which is indented.
- Remember that every transaction must have a debit equal to the credit.
- Use the third line for a short explanation of what occurred.

WORK SHEET

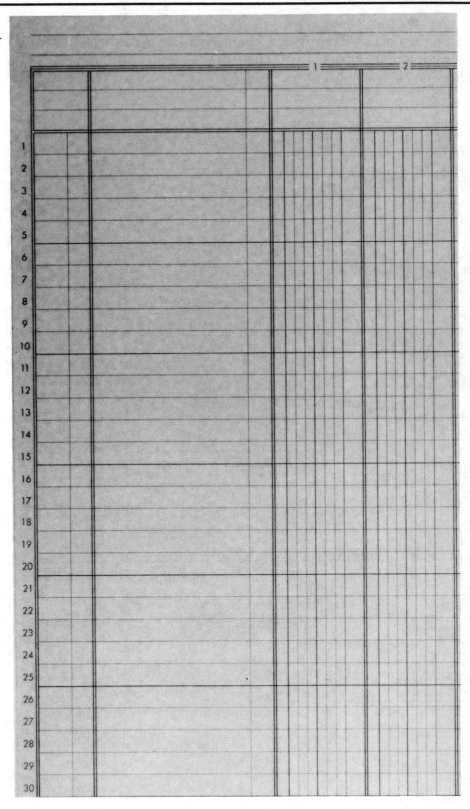

3.2 Using the work sheet provided, enter the following expenses into the journal: Rent $1,000; wages $2,000; fire insurance $800. All were paid by check on February 12, 19___.

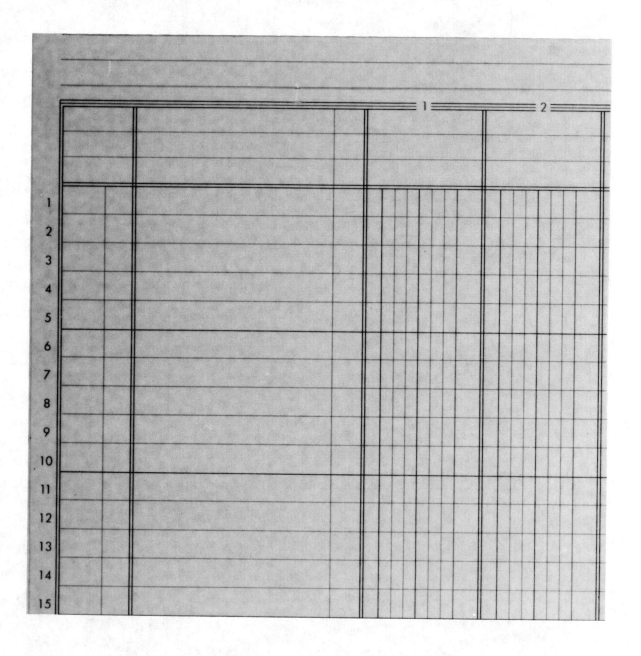

CHAPTER FOUR

The Ledger

TERMS YOU'LL NEED TO KNOW

account   *ledger*
chart of accounts   *posting*
cross-referencing   *trial balance*

When you enter transactions into the journal, they are in chronological order but otherwise mixed. Your next step is to transfer them to a **ledger,** or book of accounts, in which each individual *type* of transaction is maintained separately. This kind of record is called an **account.**

For example, a ledger has a separate page for cash transactions so that the bookkeeper can know the status of cash at all times. A separate account is kept for each customer who owes the firm money and each vendor to whom the firm owes

money. Once these accounts are established, the total of accounts receivable (what customers owe) and accounts payable (what the firm owes) can be quickly determined. In addition, a separate ledger page is created for each asset account, each type of liability, for capital, for revenue, and for expenses.

Keeping Ledger Accounts

When transactions are recorded in the journal, we speak of "entering." Transfer-

An account is set up for each customer or vendor, each type of asset and each type of liability, each revenue and expense. Entering information from the journal into these ledger pages is called *posting.*

ring information from the journal to the appropriate page in the ledger is called **posting.** Since accounts in the ledger take the form of the letter "T," they are called *ledger T accounts* (**Figure 4.1**). Ledger T accounts are similar to journal T accounts in that the left column is called the *debit* (Dr.) side and the right column is called the *credit* (Cr.) side.

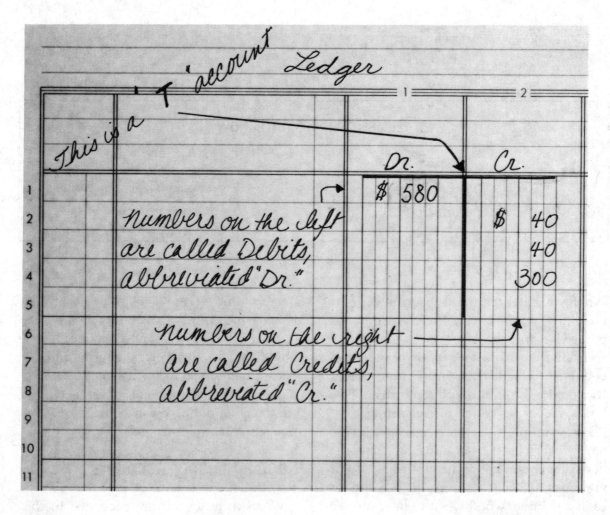

Figure 4.1

The Chart of Accounts

In their simplest form, ledger T accounts may consist of sheets in manila folders. They may be pages in a binder divided by tabs. They may be kept on computer disk files. Whatever form they take, each is assigned an *account title* and an *account number*. The title will be something like "Cash," "Payroll Account," or "Accounts Receivable, Smith Co." A single index page is kept to list all the account titles used in daily bookkeeping operations together with their numbers (**Figure 4.2**); this is called the **chart of accounts.**

CHART OF ACCOUNTS

BALANCE SHEET ACCOUNTS

   1. ASSETS

10. Cash
11. Accounts Receivable
12. Supplies on Hand
13. Merchandise
14. Office Equipment

   2. LIABILITIES

21. Accounts Payable
22. Salaries Payable
23. Taxes Payable

   3. CAPITAL

31. John Smith, Capital
32. John Smith, Drawing Account

INCOME STATEMENT ACCOUNTS

   4. REVENUES

41. Sales Revenue
42. Service Revenue

   5. EXPENSES

51. Supplies
52. Salaries
53. Rent
54. Electric
55. Telephone

Figure 4.2

Posting and Cross-Referencing

Each journal line must be separately carried forward, or posted, in its corresponding ledger account. Suppose you had a journal entry for April 6 as shown at the top of **Figure 4.3.** Your cash entry of $123 for the sale of candy would be posted as a *debit* on your cash account ledger page and a *credit* on your sales revenue account as shown in the figure.

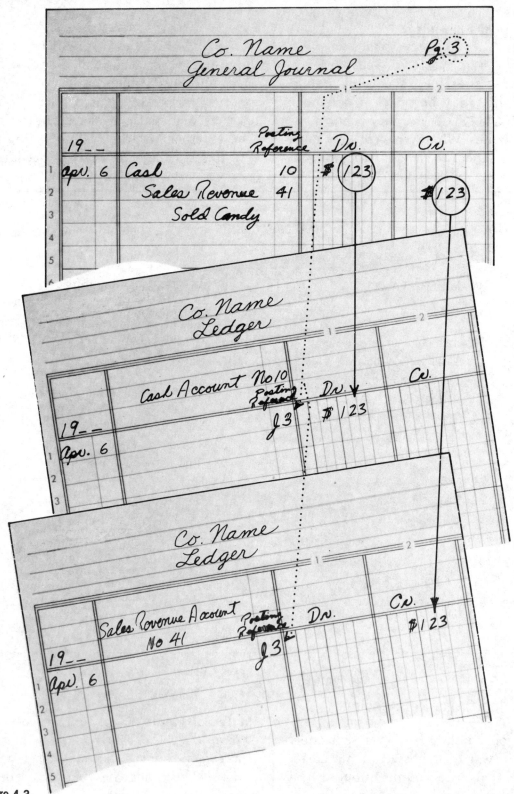

Figure 4.3

> **Locating an error later takes far more time than being precise when posting.**
> **Being precise saves time and temper.**

When you had done this, you would enter the number of the relevant account in the "posting reference" column of your journal. The number of your cash account is 10; this would appear beside the cash entry. The number of the sales revenue account is 41; this would appear beside the sales revenue entry. In the ledger, you would write "J3" in the posting reference column of both accounts to indicate where the posted item came from. This system is called **cross-referencing;** it "leaves tracks" to facilitate an audit or locate a possible error.

Your posting must be absolutely precise, because only perfect work will allow your books to balance. It is far easier to check your work as you perform it than to hunt for an error later on.

Common Errors in Posting

Several kinds of errors are common in bookkeeping; knowing what they are helps you locate them. For example, it is common to reverse numbers when writing them: 67 instead of 76. This is called a *transposition error*. All transposition errors create discrepancies that are multiples of 9. If you are out of balance and the difference between debits and credits is 9 or is evenly divisible by 9, look for a transposition error.

A *slide error* occurs when you unintentionally move a number over one place, writing $10,000 instead of $1,000 or $100,000. Of course, it is also possible to make a slide error of pennies, but a discrepancy that is a large, even number should alert you to look for a slide error.

You can also create errors by failing to post, or by posting the same number twice. Again, take care when you are posting to avoid tedious tracing of possible mistakes.

The Trial Balance

At the end of the month (or other accounting period), when every item from the journal for that period has been posted to the ledger accounts, it is time to verify that the debits and the credits in the ledger are in balance; this procedure is called the **trial balance.**

Your first step is to find the *account balance* of every ledger T account. To do this, you must:

1. Sum (add up) the debit column.
2. Sum (add up) the credit column.
3. Subtract the smaller sum from the larger.
4. Write the remainder on the larger side.

Cash Account		#10
Dr.	Cr.	
$ 50		
	$ 30	
100	___	
Balance: $ 120		

> **Transposition errors create discrepancies that are evenly divisible by 9;**
> **discrepancies that are large, even numbers are likely to be caused by slide errors.**

> At the end of each accounting period, a trial balance is cast
> to verify that the accounts have been accurately posted.

The account balance is written in smaller numbers above the line on the larger side. In the above example, $200 cash flowed into the business during the accounting period and $90 flowed out, leaving the business with $110 in cash. You can practice the account balance process in Exercise 4.3 (see page 42).

You go through the process of finding the account balance for each account in your ledger. You then make a schedule listing each account's name, number, and balance. The sum of the debit balances should equal the sum of the credit balances. A sample trial balance is shown in **Figure 4.4.**

Blue Co.
Trial Balance, June 30, 19__

Acct No.		Dr.	Cr.
10	Cash	$ 6500	
11	Accounts Receivable	12300	
12	Rent Receivable	900	
14	Inventory	23600	
21	Acc. Payable, Jones		$ 840
22	Acc. Payable, Smith Co.		1800
28	Notes Payable		5000
30	Mr. Blue, Capital		9280
40	Sales Revenue		54000
52	Supplies Expense	640	
56	Rent Expense	3000	
58	Utilities	980	
59	Salaries	23000	
		$ 70920	$ 70920

Figure 4.4

What To Do If Your Trial Balance Doesn't Balance

If your trial balance doesn't balance, going through these steps in the suggested order ensures that you will find the error in the shortest possible time.

1. Find out the exact amount of your error: by how much are you out of balance?
2. Is the error $10, $100, or $1,000? You probably failed to carry when adding or borrow when subtracting. Or you may have made a slide error in posting.
3. Look at your debits and credits. Is there an entry exactly equal to your discrepancy?
4. Does the amount of error divide evenly by 2? Look for a duplicate debit or a duplicate credit posting where there should be one of each. A debit may have been posted as a credit, or vice versa.
5. Does your out-of-balance number divide evenly by 9? Look for a transposition error or a slide.

   At this point most errors have been located.

6. Add the trial balance columns again to check for accuracy. Next, recheck the addition while looking for a misread number. Sometimes a 1 is taken for a 7, or a careless 3 or 5 may have fooled you.
7. Compare listing on the trial balance with each ledger account balance.
8. Recalculate each ledger account balance.
9. Trace each ledger posting back to its place in the journal. (Now you'll see the value of cross-referencing.) Check off each number in the ledger and in the journal as you verify it. Then look for numbers with no check mark.
10. Verify that journal debits equal the journal credits.

    If, after all this, you have not found the error, consider changing occupations. There is no other place an error could occur.

Practice Makes Perfect

In typing or piano playing, practice builds both accuracy and speed. Bookkeeping is no different. The more often you perform these procedures, the faster and more accurate you will be. To give yourself the best possible chance of being accurate:

○ Keep your workplace clean and uncluttered.
○ Concentrate; avoid noise and visual distractions.
○ Carefully check and double-check with your mind and your eyes as you write each number and during each calculation.
○ Avoid interruptions from telephone or visitors.

EXERCISES

4.1 Practice posting the journal entries in **Figure 4.5** (page 40) to the ledger accounts on the work sheet on page 41. Be sure to enter each credit and each debit and to cross-reference every time.

Smith Co.
General Journal   Pg. 7

19--		Posting Ref.	Dr.	Cr.
Apr 2	Cash		$ 3000	
	Sales Revenue			$ 3000
	Sales for Week Ended 4/2			
3	Advertising Expense		900	
	Cash			900
	Ad in Gazette			
4	Supplies on Hand		500	
	Accounts Payable, Jay Co.			500
	Purchased Supplies from Jay Co.			
9	Cash		3300	
	Sales Revenue			3300
	Sales for Week Ended 4/9			
15	Wages Expense		1400	
	Cash			1400
	Paid Wages			
30	Accounts Payable, Jay Co.		500	
	Cash			500
	Paid Supplier			

Figure 4.5

WORK SHEET

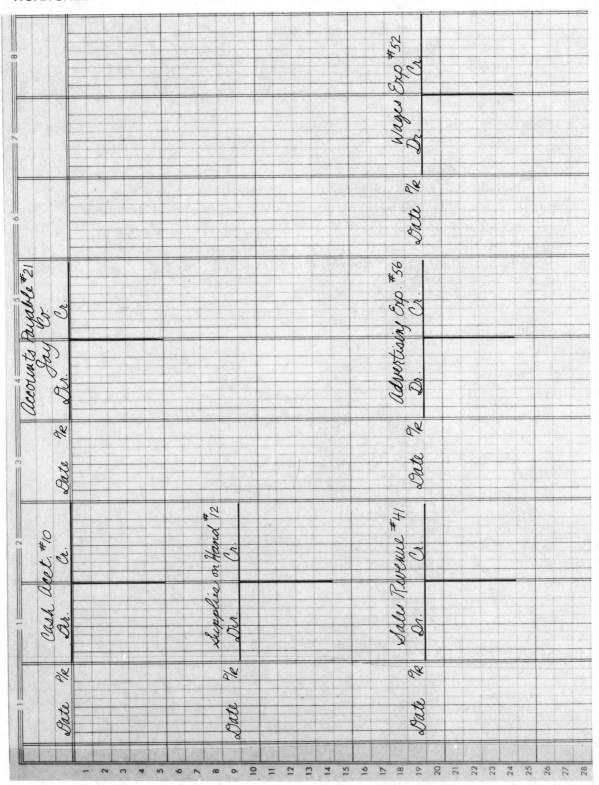

4.2 Find the account balance for the Notes Payable Account below.

Notes Payable #21

Dr.	Cr.
-0-	$9,000
$1,000	-0-
$1,000	-0-
$1,000	-0-

4.3 Using the ledger accounts you created in Exercise 4.1, prepare a trial balance. You will have to begin by writing the name of each account in a vertical column on the left side of a page. Next, find the balance in each account. List these balances as debits or credits on your page. Total the debit column and total the credit column. They should be equal.

CHAPTER FIVE

Special Journals

TERMS YOU'LL NEED TO KNOW

cash payments journal	purchases discount	sales return
cash receipts journal	purchases journal	special journals
controlling account	sales allowance	subsidiary ledger
credit memorandum	sales discount	sundry account
discounts	sales journal	trade discount

Every entry into a general journal requires at least three lines on the page: at least one debit, a credit, and a line for the explanation. If the business sold many items daily for cash or made frequent purchases of merchandise, the general journal would become crowded with entries and cumbersome to use. Special journals group common types of entries into separate journals, simplifying the process of making journal entries. One line is used instead of three, easing the bookkeeper's job. Not every item on your chart of accounts will have its own special journal; just the active or busy accounts are selected.

Special journals show both debits and credits on a single line and omit the explanation line. They are a condensed, single-purpose version of the general journal. It still remains true, though, that the total of debits will equal the total of credits.

> A *special journal* is a condensed, single-purpose version of the general journal in which a single line is used for debits and credits and the explanation line is omitted.

Types of Special Journals

Many businesses receive cash often and pay out (disburse) cash in many transactions. Therefore, it is common to have both a **cash receipts journal** and a **cash** payments journal (sometimes called a *disbursements journal*). **Figure 5.1** shows a typical cash payments journal. Compare it with the general journal shown in Figure 4.5, page 40, and note the difference in the number of lines and style of entries.

Figure 5.1

Cash Payments Journal

Date 19--	Ck. No.	Acct. Debited	Post Ref.	Acct. Pay Dr.	Sundry Acct. Dr.	Purch. Disc. Cr.	Cash Cr.
Jan 1	101	Tim Co.	✓	$ 1200			$ 1200
2	102	S. Sales Co.	✓	2300			2300
2	103	Office Salaries	70		$ 900		900
3	104	Trio, Inc.	✓	100		$ 10	90
4	105	Adv. Expense	✓	600			600
8	106	Electric Utility	75		410		410
18	107	Tri County Log	✓	1000			1000
31				$ 5200	$ 1310	$ 10	$ 6500
				(21)	(X)	(#)	(10)

In a firm where many items are purchased for inventory and eventual resale it is common to find a **purchases journal** (**Figure 5.2**). If many sales are made "on account"—that is, on credit—a **sales journal** may be maintained (**Figure 5.3**).

Figure 5.2

Purchases Journal

Date 19--	Acct. Credited	Post Ref.	Accts Pay. Cr.	Purch. Dr.	Office Supplies Dr.	Store Supplies Dr.	Sundry Accts.	Amount Dr.
Jan 1	Dale Supply	✓	$ 6200	$ 6200				
2	Bell Videotron	✓	9400	9400				
7	Off Equipt Dists.	✓	150				Office Equipt $ 150	
8	Park Co. Bros.	✓	700	700				
9	Dundee Inc.	✓	500		$ 300	$ 200		
31			$ 16950	$ 16300	$ 300	$ 200		$ 150
			(21)	(51)	(54)	(56)		(X)

Note that the entries in the purchases journal will be posted to a number of different accounts such as Accounts Payable, Office Supplies, Store Supplies, and so on. The numbers in parentheses at the base of the columns (for example, 21, 51, 54, etc. in Fig. 5.2) indicate the account numbers to which these entries are posted. The entries in the sales journal show the invoice number, the account debited, and the accounts (Sales and Accounts Receivable) to which the entries will be posted.

Figure 5.3

Sales Journal

Date	Invoice No.	Acct. Debited	Post Ref.	Accts. Rec. Dr. Sales Cr.
19--				
Jan 1	101	Barn Co.	✓	$ 9100
1	102	Salesmaster	✓	10900
2	103	Film Supply	✓	400
2	104	Cooper Bros.	✓	600
3	105	Trace Brace	✓	1000
4	106	Std. Office	✓	3100
9	107	Adler Hotel	✓	7200
19	128	Mills Bros.	✓	400
31				$ 32700
				(10) (40)

Some examples of entries in special journals are shown in Figures 5.4 through 5.7. **Figure 5.4** shows an entry in a cash receipts journal recording a transaction in which merchandise was sold for $930 in cash. This transaction results in a debit to Cash and a credit to Sales.

Figure 5.4

Sure Co.
Cash Receipts Journal

Date 19--	Acct. Credited	Post Ref.	Cash Dr.	Sales Cr.
Feb 10	Barn Co.	✓	$ 930	$ 930

Figure 5.5 shows entries for a transaction in which the business paid a vendor (the Tim Co.) for an item that had previously been charged. This transaction is a debit to Accounts Payable and a credit to Cash. (Payments made by check are recorded as cash payments.)

Figure 5.5

Date 19__	CK No.	Acct. Dr.	Post Ref.	Sundry Acct. Dr.	Accts. Payable Dr.	Purchase Discounts Cr.	Cash Cr.
Jan 1	101	Tim Co.	✓		$ 1200		$ 1200

(Sure Co. Cash Payments Journal)

In the transaction recorded in **Figure 5.6,** the business purchased $6,200 in merchandise for resale from Dale Supply. This results in a debit to Purchases and a credit to Accounts Payable.

Figure 5.6

Date 19__	Acct. Credited	Post Ref.	Acct. Pay. Cr.	Purchases Dr.	
Jan 2	Dale Supply, Inc.	✓	$ 6200	$ 6200	

(Sure Co. Purchases Journal)

When merchandise is sold on account, the transaction is recorded as a debit to Accounts Receivable and a credit to Sales. **Figure 5.7** shows that the Barn Co. purchased $9,100 worth of merchandise on credit. Note that the transaction is also debited to the customer's individual account.

Figure 5.7

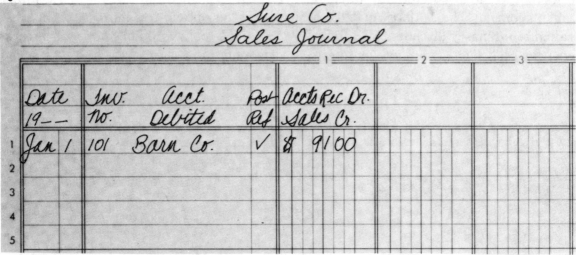

Discounts and Credit Terms

As a bookkeeper, you will be dealing with several kinds of **discounts,** or reductions from the list price of merchandise bought or sold. As a vendor (seller), your firm offers a **trade discount** to businesses that purchase its goods. Such discounts are commonly expressed as "20% [or 10%, or 50%] off list." If you made a cash sale of a $100 tape recorder at "40% off list," you would record the sale as $60 in the sales journal, ignoring the discounted amount. If you sold a $500 air conditioner to an open account (a charge customer) at a 10% discount, you would record this transaction in the sales journal (and subsequently in the ledger accounts) at $450 ($500 less $50, which is 10% of $500).

Similarly, if your firm bought the air conditioner from a vendor (wholesale supplier) at 40% off the list price of $500, you would record this transaction at $300 ($500 less $200, which is 40% of $500). You would not record the trade discount.

Terms of sale, or *credit terms*, are the terms under which a firm sells to its open account (charge) customers. Often the terms are "net 30," meaning that the account is to be paid within 30 days of purchase. After that date the account is past due, or *delinquent*.

To encourage prompt payment, many firms offer a discount—often 1% or 2%—to customers who pay within 10 days. These terms are often expressed as "2/10, n/30," meaning that the purchaser has 30 days to pay the bill but will receive a discount of 2% for paying within 10 days.

Suppose your firm, Bill Coty Leather Company, buys some heating oil from That Fuel Company on January 1 under terms of 2/10, n/30. The invoice (sales slip) total is $100, but the account will be considered paid in full if you remit $98 before January 11. **Figure 5.8** shows how this

---

When entering transactions in which goods were purchased or sold at a discount, you ignore the discount and enter the amount actually paid or received.

transaction would be entered in your cash payments journal. The $2 that you deduct is called a **purchases discount.** The bookkeeper for That Fuel Company would enter your payment in the Cash Receipts Journal as shown in **Figure 5.9.** The discount you took would be shown as a **sales discount.**

Figure 5.8

Cash Payments Journal

Date 19--	Ck No.	Acct. Debited	Post Ref	Accts Pay Dr.	Purch Disc Cr.	Cash Cr.		
Jan 6	123	That Fuel Co.	✓	$ 100	$ 2	$ 98		

Cash Receipts Journal

Date 19--	Acct. Credited	Post Ref	Accts. Rec. Cr.	Sales Disc. Dr.	Cash Dr.		
Jan 6	Bill Coty Leather	302	$ 100	$ 2	$ 98		

To summarize:
○ When the firm receives cash, *debit* Cash.
○ When a customer (outside account) pays a bill, *credit* Accounts Receivable.
○ When a customer takes a discount for prompt payment (pays less than billed), *credit* Accounts Receivable for the amount received *plus* the amount of discount legitimately taken; *debit* Sales Discounts for the discount amount; *debit* Cash only for the amount actually received.
○ Remember that "staying in balance" requires that each entry has an equality between debits and credits.

Turn to Exercise 5.1 to practice entering and posting credit sales and discounts.

> The *Sundry account* column allows you to enter unusual transactions for which there is no dedicated column in the special journal.

The Sundry Account Column

You have seen that special journals have columns reserved representing the accounts commonly posted from a particular journal. Sometimes you will encounter a situation in which no column exists for a transaction. For example, your firm may not ordinarily receive cash payments of interest. You would enter such a payment in the Sundry column (**Figure 5.10**) Transactions entered in a Sundry column are subsequently posted line by line to the appropriate ledger accounts. The total of the Sundry column is not posted.

Figure 5.10

Cash Receipts Journal
SHOWING USE OF SUNDRY COLUMN

Date 19--	Account Credited	Post Ref	Sundry Acct. Cr.	Sales Cr.	Accts. Rec. Cr.	Sales Disc. Cr.	Cash Dr.
Jan 15	Interest Income	18	$ 456				$ 456
31			$ 456				$ 456
			(X)				(10)

Turn to Exercise 5.2 to practice using Cash Payments, Purchases, and Sales special journals.

Subsidiary Ledgers and Controlling Accounts

If your firm does business on credit, you must keep accounts to show how much money each customer owes the firm and how much the firm owes each creditor. Maintaining a large number of separate accounts within the main ledger becomes burdensome. Consequently, customer and vendor accounts may be kept in alphabetical order in separate folders, binders, or computer files called **subsidiary ledgers.**

> Subsidiary ledgers of accounts receivable and accounts payable are used when a large number of customer and creditor accounts must be kept. The totals for these accounts are recorded in controlling accounts kept in the general ledger.

One subsidiary ledger would be the *accounts receivable subsidiary ledger;* the other would be your *accounts payable subsidiary ledger.*

One-page summaries of these accounts, called **controlling accounts,** are kept in the general ledger as the *accounts receivable summary account* and the *accounts payable summary account.* It is important that the sums of the balances in the subsidiary ledgers agree with the totals of the controlling accounts.

Sales Returns and Sales Allowances

Suppose a customer returns a dress to your employer's shop because it does not match the jacket she planned to wear with it. You would refund her money, and the transaction would be called a **sales return.** Or perhaps a customer notices that a button is missing from a dress on display, and she is given a price reduction; this is called a **sales allowance.** Both sales returns and sales allowances are reductions to sales revenue. If a cash refund is given, the sales returns and allowances account must be debited and the cash account must be credited. If the item being returned was sold on credit, accounts receivable must be credited, and the customer's account must be credited in both the subsidiary ledger for accounts receivable and the control account.

A sales allowance may be handled like a discount. A credit sales return, however, generally requires that a **credit memorandum** be issued to document the amount that was credited to the customer's account. This may be a credit slip similar to a sales slip, or it may be a notice sent through the mail. The recipient may attach the credit memorandum to the next payment in place of a check for the amount due.

Handling Sales Tax

Most states charge purchasers a sales tax stated as a percentage of the sale and require sellers to collect it. The seller's bookkeeper will credit Sales Tax Payable, a liability account, for the amount of the tax.

For example, on a charge sale of $100 in a state with a 6% tax rate, the buyer would be billed for $106 ($100 plus $6 tax). When payment is made, the bookkeeper debits accounts receivable for the full amount of $106, credits sales for $100, and credits Sales Tax Payable for $6. When the sales tax is paid to the state, the transaction is recorded as a debit to Sales Tax Payable and a credit to Cash. Computers have greatly speeded up and simplified the accounting of sales taxes, but the principles regarding where debits and credits are entered remain the same.

EXERCISES

5.1 Using the work sheet provided (**Figure 5.11**), enter the following transactions. After you post the items to the work sheet, verify that the sum of all debits equals the sum of all credits. (Remember that in actuality you would post items for the entire month or whatever accounting period you were using before computing totals and balancing your accounts.)

Aug. 1: Received payment on account of $2,000 from R. Brown.

Aug. 1: Received payment on account of $490 from Blue & Sons in which a discount of 2% was taken from the $500 invoice.

Aug. 1: Received $1,600 from sales.

Aug. 2: Received payment on account of $900 from L. Hamilton on which a 10% discount was taken from the $1,000 invoice.

Aug. 2: Received $750 cash service revenue.

Aug. 3: Received $90 from T. Gallagher in full payment of July bill.

Figure 5.11

Date	Acct. Cr.	Post Ref	Sundry Acct. Cr.	Sales Cr.	Accts. Rec. Cr.	Sales Disc. Dr.	Cash Dr.

5.2 Use the work sheets (**Figure 5.12**) to enter the following transactions:

Sept. 1: You (your firm) purchased $1,200 in goods, paying by check (a cash purchase).

Sept. 1: You paid Volt Electric Company $980 after taking 2% off the purchase invoice of $1,000.

Sept. 2: You paid salaries of $800.

Sept. 2: You purchased $3,000 in merchandise on credit from A-V Electronics.

Sept. 3: You sold merchandise on account to Ramco for $9,000.

Sept. 3: You paid Winston Brothers the $600 owed them but took an allowed 10% discount and wrote the check for $540.

Sept. 4: Credit sales were $370.

Sept. 5: You purchased $200 in merchandise from Disk Company, paying $150 after discount.

Sept. 6: You paid advertising expense of $95.

Sept. 7: You sold the firm's old typewriter for $50 and sent an invoice.

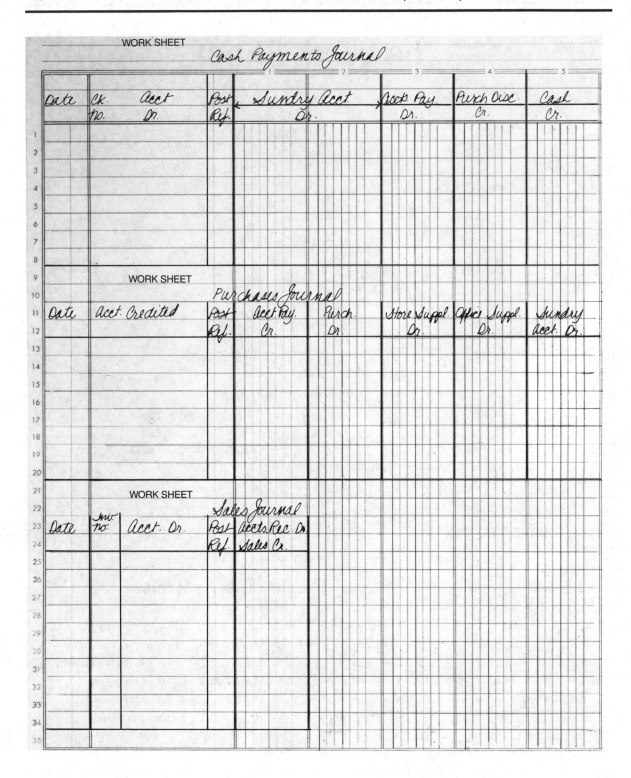

Figure 5.12

CHAPTER SIX

The Work Sheet

TERMS YOU'LL NEED TO KNOW

adjusted trial balance
adjustments to journal entries
contra asset

unadjusted trial balance
work sheet

You have now learned several of the procedural steps of a bookkeeper's job: (1) Making a journal entry for each transaction, (2) posting journal entries to ledger accounts, and (3) making a trial balance. You also learned how special journals and subsidiary accounts fit into these procedures. These steps basically consisted of gathering and recording data. Now you will begin readying these figures to use in financial statements that will be presented to the owners and managers of the business to assist them in planning.

Using The Work Sheet

Before you can make final financial reports for the accounting period, you will need to make changes or **adjustments** in your trial balance figures to allow for situations and events that were not recorded in the day-to-day entries and postings. For example, if you have not been making a change in your office supply ledger account each time a supply is used (which would be impractical in most cases), you will now have to take an inventory count

> The *work sheet* is not a final report but rather a tool to ensure accuracy and completeness when the financial statements are compiled.

of your office supplies to see the value of what you actually have on hand and adjust the account balance accordingly.

Furthermore, machinery and buildings wear out (depreciate), and an adjustment for depreciation must be made to your capital asset accounts. (Depreciation is explained in Chapter 10.) You may owe wages, salaries, or commissions that have not yet shown on these expense accounts because they have not yet been paid. The books may need to recognize that some accounts receivable will never be collected.

The bookkeeper must take the initiative here, because unlike transactions, adjustments are not usually supported by paper documentation. You may have to request information from others in the firm, take inventories, or consult records from prior years to see what kinds of adjustments are generally required.

The **work sheet** simplifies making these adjustments and checking them for accuracy. It reduces the likelihood of errors in the final reports and simplifies preparing them. The work sheet itself is not a formal report, nor is it presented to anyone. Usually it is prepared in pencil.

Setting Up Your Work Sheet

Generally, the work sheet has ten columns, consisting of a debit (Dr) column and a credit (Cr) column for each of five categories:

○ Unadjusted Trial Balance
○ Adjustments
○ Adjusted Trial Balance
○ Income (Operating) Statement
○ Balance Sheet

Some bookkeepers omit columns 7 and 8. We will discuss each of these categories in turn.

Columns 1 and 2 (Unadjusted Trial Balance)

You begin your work sheet by copying the trial balance data into columns 1 and 2 of the work sheet (**Figure 6.1**). At this point, some of the balances shown will be incorrect, not because of errors but because adjustments must be made (usually at year's end) to update some figures. For this reason, columns 1 and 2 are labeled "Unadjusted Trial Balance."

Columns 3 and 4: Adjustments to Trial Balance

Adjustments to the trial balances are first entered on the appropriate line in columns 3 and 4. Suppose you started the month (or other accounting period) with $2,200 worth of office supplies available for use. Now, at the end of the period, you

Figure 6.1

Office Aid Co.
Work Sheet
March 31, 19__

Acct. No.	Account Name	Unadjusted Trial Balance Dr.	Unadjusted Trial Balance Cr.
10	Cash	$ 4100	
11	Accounts Rec.	5200	
12	Office Supplies	2200	
13	Furniture + Fixtures	20000	
14	Accumulated Depr.		$ 6500
21	Accounts Payable		2800
31	Capital Stock		10000
38	Retained Earnings 3/31		7400
40	Service Revenue		60000
52	Salaries Expense	49000	
53	Utilities Expense	1200	
58	Rent Expense	5000	
		$ 86700	$ 86700

have taken an inventory and found that only $1,200 worth of office supplies remain on the shelves. By subtracting $1,200 (the amount remaining) from $2,200 (the trial balance amount for the Office Supplies account), you find that $1,000 in supplies has been consumed in day-to-day use that was not recorded. You must adjust your trial balance to reflect this $1,000 change, which will eventually be shown on the operating statement as an office supplies expense.

Figure 6.2 shows how these adjustments

are made. The Office Supplies account has been credited in column 4 and debited in column 3. These paired adjustments are marked with a lower-case "a" in parentheses so that they can be matched up when the work sheet is read. Later, you will identify other paired adjustments as (b), (c), and so on. The *debit* in column 3, line 14, shows a $1,000 office supplies expense, which must be *credited* to office supplies in column 4, line 3 to reduce this account.

Now, suppose you learn that rent in the

Figure 6.2

Office Aid Co.
Work Sheet
March 31, 19__

	Acct. No.	Account Name	Unadjusted Trial Balance Dr.	Cr.	Adjustments Dr.	Cr.
1	10	Cash	$ 4100			
2	11	Accounts Rec.	5200			
3	12	Office Supplies	2200			(a) 1000
4	13	Furniture + Fixtures	20000			
5	14	Accumulated Depr.		$ 6500		
6	21	Accounts Payable		2800		
7	31	Capital Stock		10000		
8	38	Retained Earnings 3/31		7400		
9	40	Service Revenue		60000		
10	52	Salaries Expense	49000			
11	53	Utilities Expense	1200			
12	58	Rent Expense	5000			
13			$ 86700	$ 86700		
14	57	Supplies Expense			(a) 1000	
15						

amount of $400 is due. It has not been journalized, since it has not yet been paid, but it will be an expense for the period in question. **Figure 6.3** shows that a *debit* in column 3, line 12 has increased rent expense by $400 and is matched with a *credit* to accounts payable in column 4, line 6. These paired adjustments are labeled (b).

Figure 6.3

Office Aid Co.
Work Sheet
March 31, 19__

	Acct. No.	Account Name	Unadjusted Trial Balance Dr.	Cr.	Adjustments Dr.	Cr.
1	10	Cash	$ 4100			
2	11	Accounts Rec.	5200			
3	12	Office Supplies	2200			(a) 1000
4	13	Furniture + Fixtures	20000			
5	14	Accumulated Depr.		$ 6500		
6	21	Accounts Payable		2800		(b) 400
7	31	Capital Stock		10000		
8	38	Retained Earnings 3/31		7400		
9	40	Service Revenue		60000		
10	52	Salaries Expense	49000			
11	53	Utilities Expense	1200			
12	58	Rent Expense	5000		(b) 400	
13			$ 86700	$ 86700		
14	57	Supplies Expense			(a) 1000	
15						

You now turn to the issue of depreciation. The depreciation calculated for furniture and fixtures for the period (see Chapter 10) is $500. This is shown as a *debit* in column 3, line 15 and a *credit* to accumulated depreciation in column 4, line 5 (**Figure 6.4**). These entries are labeled (c).

Acct. No.	Account Name	Unadjusted Trial Balance Dr.	Cr.	Adjustments Dr.	Cr.
10	Cash	$ 4100			
11	Accounts Rec.	5200			
12	Office Supplies	2200			(a) 1000
13	Furniture + Fixtures	20000			
14	Accumulated Depr.		$ 6500		(c) 500
21	Accounts Payable		2800		(d) 400
31	Capital Stock		10000		
38	Retained Earnings 3/31		7400		
40	Service Revenue		60000		
52	Salaries Expense	49000			
53	Utilities Expense	1200			
58	Rent Expense	5000		(d) 400	
		$ 86700	$ 86700		
57	Office Supplies Expense			(a) 1000	
59	Depreciation Expense			(c) 500	

Figure 6.4

Finally, you learn that as of the last day of the accounting period, several days' pay will be due to the employees, amounting to $2,600. To reflect reality, a salaries expense must be shown as a *debit*, and a liability called Salaries Payable must be *credited* with this amount. These adjustments are identified as (d) in **Figure 6.5**.

Office Aid Co.
Work Sheet
March 31, 19___

Acct. No.	Account Name	Unadjusted Trial Balance Dr.	Cr.	Adjustments Dr.	Cr.
10	Cash	$ 4100			
11	Accounts Rec.	5200			
12	Office Supplies	2200			(a) 1000
13	Furniture + Fixtures	20000			
14	Accumulated Depr.		$ 6500		(c) 500
21	Accounts Payable		2800		(b) 400
31	Capital Stock		10000		
38	Retained Earnings 3/31		7400		
40	Service Revenue		60000		
52	Salaries Expense	49000		(d) 2600	
53	Utilities Expense	1200			
58	Rent Expense	5000		(b) 400	
		$ 86700	$ 86700		
57	Office Supplies Expense			(a) 1000	
59	Depreciation Expense			(c) 500	
24	Salaries Payable				(d) 2600
				$ 4500	$ 4500

Figure 6.5

Columns 5 and 6: Adjusted Trial Balance

When you have entered all the necessary adjustments in columns 3 and 4, it is time to extend the totals to arrive at your adjusted trial balance in columns 5 and 6. If no adjustment was necessary for an account, you simply bring the amounts from columns 1 and 2 over into columns 5 and 6. But if, for example, there is a credit in column 1 and a debit in column 4, you must *subtract* one from the other and enter the result, whether a debit or credit, in column 5 or 6, respectively. **Figure 6.6** shows how this is done for office supplies (line 3).

Office Aid Co.
Work Sheet
March 31, 19—

	Acct. No.	Account Name	Trial Balance Dr.	Trial Balance Cr.	Adjustments Dr.		Adjustments Cr.		Adjusted Trial Balance Dr.	Adjusted Trial Balance Cr.
1	10	Cash	$ 4100						$ 4100	
2	11	Accounts Rec.	5200						5200	
3	12	Office Supplies	2200				(a)	1000	1200	
4	13	Furniture + Fixtures	20000						20000	
5	14	Accumulated Depr.		$ 6500			(c)	500		$ 7000
6	21	Accounts Payable		2800			(b)	400		3200
7	31	Capital Stock		10000						10000
8	38	Retained Earnings 3/31		7400						7400
9	40	Service Revenue		60000						60000
10	52	Salaries Expense	49000		(d)	2600			51600	
11	53	Utilities Expense	1200						1200	
12	58	Rent Expense	5000		(b)	400			5400	
13			$ 86700	$ 86700						
14	57	Office Supplies Expense			(a)	1000			1000	
15	59	Depreciation Expense			(c)	500			500	
16	24	Salaries Payable					(d)	2600		2600
17					$ 4500		$ 4500		$ 90200	$ 90200
18										
19										
20										

Figure 6.6

If column 2 and column 4 both show credits, these must be added and the sum carried into column 6 as shown on lines 5 and 6 of Figure 6.6. If there is a debit in column 1 and an adjustment debit in column 3, these are *added* and the sum put into column 5 (the adjusted debit column)—see line 10 of Figure 6.6.

To verify that you have performed these steps correctly, add up the columns. Columns 3 and 4 should be equal, and so should columns 5 and 6. If they are not, check your work on each line before proceeding.

Don't despair! The steps just described seem confusing, but with careful attention and practice they become routine. Persevere at this point, and you will gain a valuable career skill. Don't allow yourself to be overwhelmed: Continue.

Columns 7 and 8: Operating Statement Items

Now you are preparing information that you will use in computing the Operating Statement (Chapter 7). At this point it is useful to use a straightedge such as a ruler to guide your eye along the lines. Focus on your adjusted trial balance col-

> **Accounts that normally have credit balances are placed in column 8;
> accounts that normally have debit (minus) balances are placed in column 7.**

umns (columns 5 and 6). Line by line, select *only revenue and expense items* and enter them in columns 7 and 8 according to whether they are debit or credit items.

Revenue accounts such as Sales Revenue or Service Revenue normally have credit balances. Depending on the nature of the business, these may include Interest Revenue, Rental Revenue, and so on. These are placed in column 8.

Expense items normally have debit balances. Selected items such as Salaries Expense, Utilities Expense, Supplies Expense, and so on are placed as adjusted trial balances in column 7. These procedures are shown in **Figure 6.7.**

Office Aid Co.
Work Sheet
March 31, 19__

Acct. No.	Account Name	Unadjusted Trial Balance Dr.	Cr.	Adjustments Dr.	Cr.	Adjusted Trial Balance Dr.	Cr.	Income Statement Dr.	Cr.
10	Cash	$ 4100				$ 4100			
11	Accounts Rec.	5200				5200			
12	Office Supplies	2200			(a) 1000	1200			
13	Furniture + Fixtures	20000				20000			
14	Accumulated Dep.		$ 6500		(c) 500		$ 7000		
21	Accounts Payable		2800		(b) 400		3200		
31	Capital Stock		10000				10000		
38	Retained Earnings 3/31		7400				7400		
40	Service Revenue		60000				60000		$ 60000
52	Salaries Expense	49000		(d) 2600		51600		$ 51600	
53	Utilities Expense	1200				1200		1200	
58	Rent Expense	5000		(b) 400		5400		5400	
		$ 86700	$ 86700						
57	Office Supplies Expense			(a) 1000		1000		1000	
59	Depreciation Expense			(c) 500		500		500	
24	Salaries Payable				(d) 2600		2600		
				$ 4500	$ 4500	$ 90200	$ 90200	$ 59700	$ 60000

Figure 6.7

If you decide to add columns 7 and 8, do not expect the debits and credits to be equal. *Inequality is normal here.*

Columns 9 and 10: Balance Sheet Items

Once you have transferred all revenue and expense items to columns 7 and 8, the remaining items will pertain to assets, liabilities, and capital. Now you are entering information you will use in preparing the balance sheet for the period (see Chapter 7).

The items will consist of Cash, Accounts Receivable, Supplies, Furniture and Fixtures, Machinery, Land and Buildings, and any other property of value. The normal account balance for these is a *debit*, so they are put into column 9. Accumulated Depreciation is called a **contra asset** because it applied against capital assets; it is entered as a credit to column 10. Liability accounts such as Accounts Payable or Salaries Payable normally have credit balances and are entered in column 10. The results of these entries are shown in **Figure 6.8.** Take care not to omit any items that have been written in, such as Salaries Payable on line 16.

Office Aid Co.
Work Sheet
March 31, 19—

	Acct. No.	Account Name	Unadjusted Trial Balance Dr.	Cr.	Adjustments Dr.	Cr.	Adjusted Trial Balance Dr.	Cr.	Income Statement Dr.	Cr.	Balance Sheet Dr.	Cr.
1	10	Cash	$ 4100				$ 4100				$ 4100	
2	11	Accounts Rec.	5200				5200				5200	
3	12	Office Supplies	2200			(a) $ 1000	1200				1200	
4	13	Furniture + Fixture	20000				20000				20000	
5	14	Accumulated Depr.		$ 6500		(c) 500		$ 7000				$ 7000
6	21	Accounts Payable		2800		(b) 400		3200				3200
7	31	Capital Stock		10000				10000				10000
8	38	Retained Earnings 3/31		7400				7400				7400
9	40	Service Revenue		60000				60000		$ 60000		
10	52	Salaries Expense	49000		(d) $ 2600		51600		$ 51600			
11	53	Utilities Expense	1200				1200		1200			
12	58	Rent Expense	5000		(b) 400		5400		5400			
13			$ 86700	$ 86700								
14	57	Office Supplies Expense			(a) 1000		1000		1000			
15	59	Depreciation Expense			(c) 500		500		500			
16	24	Salaries Payable				(d) 2600		2600				2600
17					$ 4500	$ 4500	$ 90200	$ 90200	$ 59700	$ 60000	$ 30500	$ 30200
18		Net Income (Loss)							300			300

Figure 6.8

Total columns 7, 8, 9, and 10. For columns 7 and 8, subtract the smaller total from the larger one and write in the difference below the smaller total.

○ If the total for column 8 is larger than that for column 7, the business shows a profit in the amount of the difference.

○ If column 7 totals more than column 8, the business shows a loss in the amount of the difference.

○ If column 9 totals more than column 10, the owners' equity (capital) has increased during the accounting period by the amount of the difference.

○ If column 10 totals more than column 9, the owners' equity has decreased during the accounting period by the amount of the difference.

Verifying Your Accuracy

The difference between columns 7 and 8 should be equal to the difference between columns 9 and 10. If the differences are not equal, check your work. Notice that in Figure 6.8, the $300 at the bottom of column 7 equals the $300 near the bottom of column 10. The business has shown a net income or profit of $300 for this period, and the owners' equity has increased by that amount.

> The amount of profit or loss for the period should equal the increase or decrease, respectively, of the owners' equity (capital) for the period.

Journalizing the Adjustment Entries

To complete your work sheet, you will now need to enter each adjustment in the general journal. These are the items (a), (b), and so forth in columns 3 and 4 of Figure 6.8. For the entries made in this chapter, you would need to make the following **adjustments to journal entries:**

General Journal

	Dr.	Cr.
Adjusting Entries		
Supplies Expense	$1,000	
Supplies		$1,000
Rent Expense	400	
Accounts Payable		400
Depreciating Expense	500	
Accumulated Depreciation		500
Salaries Expense	2,600	
Salaries Payable		2,600

In adjusting journal entries, follow these three rules:

1. To adjust a prepaid item that has been consumed through the passage of time, increase the expense with a debit and decrease the asset with a credit:
   Example:
   Rent Expense . . . . . Dr.
      Prepaid Rent . . . . Cr.

2. To adjust a payable, increase the expense with a debit and increase the payable with a credit.

   Example:
   Salaries Expense . . . . . Dr.
      Salaries Payable . . . . Cr.

3. To show depreciation adjustment, increase the expense with a debit and increase accumulated depreciation with a credit.

    Example:

    Depreciation Expense . . . . . Dr.
      Accumulated Depreciation . . . . . Cr.

When you have completed the ten-column work sheet, you will be able to create an operating statement and a balance sheet with ease, as you will see in Chapter 7.

EXERCISE

6.1 Create a ten-column work sheet for the Select Sheet Company, using the information provided. After entering the trial balance in columns 1 and 2, record the following adjustments:

(a) Inventory of supplies on hand now shows $400.
(b) The prepaid rent has now been used.
(c) Depreciation for the month is $400.
(d) Salaries in the amount of $1,000 are now payable.

	Dr.	Cr.
Cash	$3,000	
Accounts Receivable	2,000	
Office Supplies	2,400	
Prepaid Rent	1,200	
Tools & Equipment	1,000	
Accumulated Depreciation		$500
Accounts Payable		800
John Trout, Capital		6,500
John Trout, Drawing	3,000	
Sales		16,000
Salary Expense	11,000	
Miscellaneous Expenses	200	

6.2 Now use a separate piece of accounting paper to journalize the adjustments you have made in Exercise 6.1.

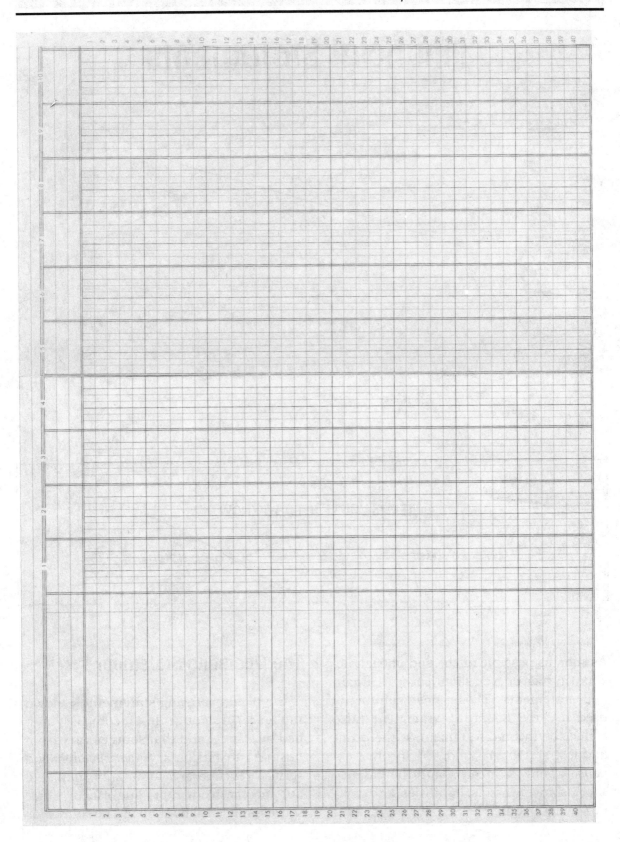

Financial Statements

As soon as possible at the end of each accounting period, you should prepare financial statements. Those most commonly used are the **operating statement** (also called the income statement or the profit and loss statement), showing income, expenses, and net income, and the **balance sheet,** showing assets, liabilities, and capital (owners' equity).

The Operating Statement

A typical operating statement is shown in **Figure 7.1.** Notice that income is classified by source, and that sources vary from business to business. Sales revenue and service revenue are commonly included, but income from rent, interest, or other sources may also be shown. The source for the operating statement is your work sheet; simply enter columns 7 and 8 from the work sheet into the appropriate layout as shown in the figure.

Figure 7.1

SAMPLE COMPANY
Operating Statement
Year Ended December 31, 19____

INCOME

Sales Revenue	$250,000	
Service Revenue	150,000	
Total Revenues		$400,000
Less Cost of Goods Sold		$125,000
Gross Profit		$275,000

EXPENSES

Wages & Salaries	120,000	
Rent	100,000	
Utilities	15,000	
Advertising	2,000	
Insurance	2,000	
Depreciation	1,000	
Supplies	500	
Repairs	400	
Licenses	100	
Bad Debts	100	
Total Expenses		$241,100
NET INCOME		$ 33,900

Expenses are listed below income. Customarily they are listed in declining order of value, although the owners of the business may prefer some other arrangement.

Net income, which appears on the bottom line and is often so called, represents the earnings of the company—its profit. Sometimes net income represents earnings before federal corporate income taxes are computed (net profit before taxes), and another computation is made in which taxes are subtracted (net profit after taxes). For a proprietorship not subject to corporate income taxes, net income and profit would be the same.

In seasonal businesses especially, only the year-end accounting will truly convey the profitability of the business. Building contractors and farmers, for example, often show a loss in the first quarter of the year, and retail stores may count on making all or most of their profit in the final quarter.

Rules Regarding Format

Refer back to Figure 7.1 with particular attention to its format, especially indentions and the location of dollar signs and underlining. Bookkeepers differentiate between records kept in dollars and those using other measurements such as weight or units sold. Someone unfamiliar with a particular document can tell at a glance whether it is a financial accounting. The rules for dollar signs are:

○ Place a $ at the top of each column representing money.
○ Use a $ after every addition or subtraction, that is, next to every total or result representing money.

Similarly, there are conventions regarding underlining that convey information at a glance.

Net income, or the "bottom line," tells the owners of the business whether their efforts are profitable.

> The operating statement answers the question "Did we make a profit?"
> The balance sheet answers the question, "What financial shape are we in?"

○ A line is drawn beneath any column that is to be added or subtracted.
○ Every final total sum is underscored twice.

Resist the temptation to be hasty; don't underscore freehand, but give your work a professional appearance by using a straightedge. Use a pencil with a very sharp point, not a dull point, and never a pen. Even the best bookkeepers are subject to occasional mistakes. Pencil lines can be erased neatly; ink cannot.

A word on operating statements produced by computer: Now is the time to put a fresh ribbon into the printer. Not only will the statement make a better impression, but photocopies distributed—say, to management or to the bank—will be easy to read.

The Balance Sheet

The operating statement shows how much the firm has earned (or lost) during the accounting period. The balance sheet shows the cumulative effect of the firm's operations on the financial position of the owners. To make up the balance sheet for your firm, you will use columns 9 and 10 of your work sheet.

Figure 7.2 shows a typical balance sheet. Note that while the operating statement follows the formula R minus E equals NI, the balance sheet must balance.

Figure 7.2

SAMPLE COMPANY
Balance Sheet
December 31, 19____

ASSETS			LIABILITIES		
CURRENT ASSETS			CURRENT LIABILITIES		
Cash	$12,000				
Accounts Receivable	24,000		Accounts Payable	$6,500	
Inventory	10,000		Note Payable	5,000	
Total Current Assets		$46,000	Total Current Liability		$11,500
PLANT ASSETS			LONG-TERM LIABILITIES		
Equipment	$11,000		Mortgage Payable	$30,000	
Less Accumulated Depreciation	1,000		Total Long-Term		
Total Plant Assets		$10,000	Liabilities		$30,000
			TOTAL LIABILITIES		$41,500
			OWNER'S EQUITY		
			J. Sample, Capital		$14,500
TOTAL ASSETS		$56,000	TOTAL LIABILITIES & CAPITAL		$56,000

Study the *groupings* in Figure 7.2. "Assets" (listed on the left) groups current assets and shows their total, then lists plant assets and shows their total. Note also that the amount of cumulative depreciation is shown on the balance sheet as a deduction from the original value of the equipment.

"Liabilities" (listed on the right) first lists current liabilities, then long-term liabilities, then total liabilities. The owners' equity (capital) is arrived at with the formula $A - L = C$ and entered beneath the total liabilities (which represent the creditors' equity).

Although you will initially make up both the operating statement and the balance sheet manually (unless you are using a computer program), most businesses require that the financial statements be finalized in typewritten form. The accounting manager or the controller, if the business is large enough to have one, will make a final check for accuracy before the typewritten statements are prepared.

Only one more step remains in the accounting cycle before it starts all over again. That step is to prepare the books for the upcoming accounting period. Closing the books is discussed in Chapter 8.

EXERCISE

7.1 Using the information on the work sheet for Exercise 6.1 (see the Solutions section), prepare an operating statement and a balance sheet for the Select Sheet Company. Use the forms provided here.

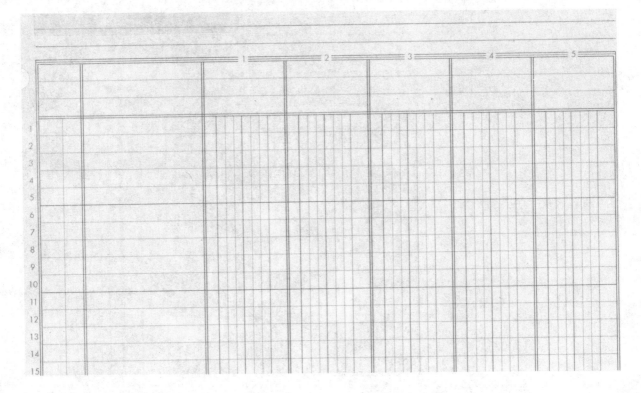

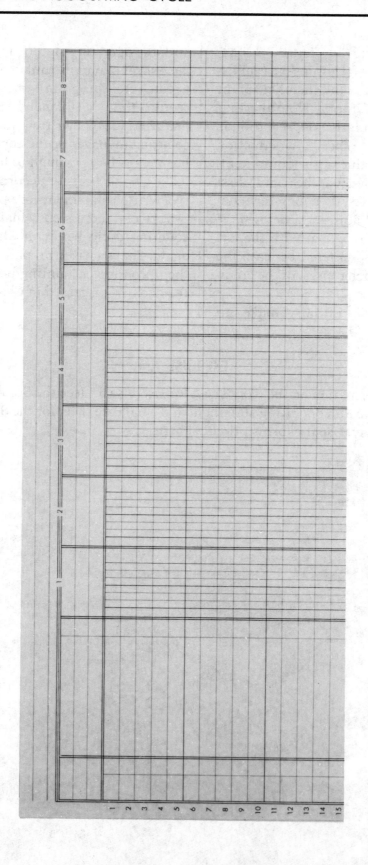

CHAPTER EIGHT

Closing the Books

TERMS YOU'LL NEED TO KNOW

drawing account   *income summary*   *post-closing trial balance*

Your final task in the accounting cycle is to close the books: to ready each revenue and expense account for the next accounting period, to adjust the capital (owners' equity) account by the amount of the profit or loss incurred in the previous period, and to adjust the capital account to reflect money drawn by the owner for personal use.

The Drawing Account

Withdrawal

The **drawing account** is the ledger account in which you record money the owner has withdrawn for his or her personal use. The ledger sheet is headed with the owner's name followed by the word "drawing"; for example, "John Smith, Drawing." For each sum drawn by the

---

**Money drawn by the owner(s) for personal use is recorded
in a drawing account and charged against capital.**

owner, you *credit* Cash and *debit* the drawing account. When the accounts are closed, the debit balance in the drawing account is charged against capital.

The Income Summary

You begin the process of closing after you have journalized every adjusting entry from columns 3 and 4 of your work sheet (see Chapter 7). A new T account called the **income summary** is created to summarize the information from all revenue and expense accounts. The closing process then consists of the following steps (**Figure 8.1**):

1. *Bringing revenue accounts to zero.* You *debit* each revenue account in the ledger in the amount of its balance, bringing the accounts to zero and readying them to receive the revenue of the next bookkeeping period. You

1. Revenue Accounts

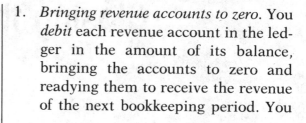

2. Expense Accounts

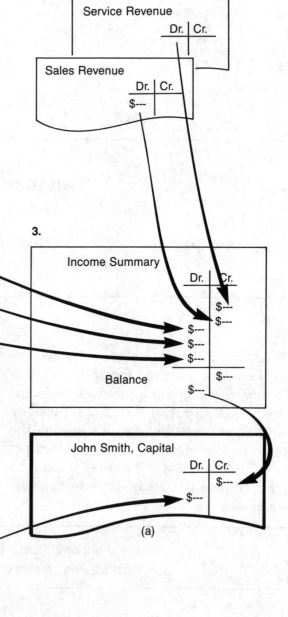

Figure 8.1

then *credit* the income summary with the total of all revenues.

2. *Bringing expense accounts to zero.* You *credit* each expense account in the amount of its balance, bringing it to zero and readying it for the next bookkeeping period. You then *debit* the income summary by the total of all expenses.

3. *Balancing the income summary and adjusting the capital account.* You find the balance in the income summary account (add the debit and the credit). If the firm has made a profit, you will have a credit balance. You *debit* the income summary by this amount and *credit* the capital account. A debit (minus) balance in the income summary account shows that the business has incurred a loss. You *credit* the income summary for that amount and *debit* the capital account.

4. *Adjusting for the owner's "draw."* You *credit* the drawing account in the amount of its balance (total) and *debit* the capital account in the same amount as previously described.

You would conclude the closing process by making journal entries for each step. The result would look like **Figure 8.2.**

The foregoing description assumes the business is a proprietorship. In a corporation, you would have a Dividends account (showing dividends paid to stockholders) in addition to the Income Summary. Both these accounts would be closed to the Retained Earnings account (see Chapter 16).

Figure 8.2

General Journal
Closing Entries

19____		Dr.	Cr.
Dec. 31	Sales Revenue	$98,000	
	Income Summary		$98,000
31	Income Summary	88,000	
	Rent Expense		30,000
	Wages Expense		40,000
	Utilities		12,000
	Depreciation Expense		6,000
31	Income Summary	10,000	
	John Smith, Capital		10,000
31	John Smith, Capital	2,100	
	John Smith, Drawing Acct.		2,100

The Post-Closing Trial Balance

It is customary to take a **post-closing trial balance** to verify the accuracy of the closing process. After completing all the steps of closing, you list the balances in each ledger account (before they were brought to zero) in two columns, Dr. and Cr. The sum of the debits should equal the sum of the credits. At this point the accounting cycle is completed.

A Word About Correcting Errors

Errors do occur; that is why a pencil is used in bookkeeping instead of the more permanent ink. However, erasures may raise questions about why the change was made. The better way is to draw a single ruled line through the incorrect number, writing the accurate amount directly above. This method shows clearly why a number was changed and promotes bookkeeping with integrity.

PART THREE

SPECIALIZED PROCEDURES

Merchandising Accounts

Most small businesses are in one of two categories: service (beauty or barber shops, bookkeeping or accounting firms, real estate firms) or sales (hardware stores, liquor stores, furniture stores). Retailers, also called merchandisers, buy goods at wholesale and sell them to consumers; they maintain a stock, or inventory, of goods for sale. (Service firms may sell some goods, just as retailers may provide some services; the discussion in this chapter pertains to the retail aspect of any firm.) Certain journal entries and calculations are primarily performed in merchandising operations: sales returns, purchase discounts, and inventory.

Certain calculations affect mainly merchandising operations: sales returns, purchase discounts, and inventory.

The bookkeeper for a merchandising firm must compute the **cost of goods** sold as part of the operating statement. Goods returned must also be accounted for. Gross (total) revenues less returns equals **net sales,** or *net* customer *purchases*. A simplified operating statement for a merchandising firm showing calculations to this point is shown in **Figure 9.1**

The gross profit figure is used to calculate the **operating margin** of the business, which is computed by dividing the gross profit on sales by the gross sales. The result will be the percentage by which goods must be marked up to cover their actual cost. However, the operating statement at this point does not account for stock remaining on hand for sale (**inventory**), which must be added back in to determine **gross profit.** The remaining expenses of the business are then totaled and deducted in the usual fashion to arrive at the net income.

Inventory

Basically, **inventory** means the stock goods on hand for sale. However, in determining the value of inventory at the end of an accounting period, the amount on hand at the beginning must be known, the value of goods purchased during the accounting period must be added, and the value of goods sold or shipped back must be subtracted.

Figure 9.2 shows how adjustments for inventory and returns are made in calculating the cost of goods sold. Note that a value must be assigned to the inventory in order to make this computation.

BETTY'S BOOTERY
Operating Statement
for the Month Ending Dec. 31, 19___

REVENUE	
Gross Sales	$75,800
Less Sales Returns	800
Net Sales	$75,000
Less Cost of Goods Sold	45,000
Gross Profit on Sales	$30,000

Figure 9.1

In calculating the cost of goods sold, the value of goods on hand, or inventory, must be computed.

Beginning Inventory		$40,000
Purchases	$21,000	
Less Purchase Returns	1,000	
Net Purchases		$20,000
Merchandise Available for Sale		$60,000
Less Ending Inventory		15,000
Cost of Goods Sold		$45,000

Figure 9.2

Computing the Value of Inventory

The inventory value is computed by counting the goods and then assigning a value to them. Sometimes an actual physical count is done only at the end of the year or quarter; interim counts are approximated from records of purchase and sale. (Computer programs can be designed to accomplish this.) Physical inventory—counting items and adding up price tags—helps determine how much is being lost through shoplifting or employee pilferage and provides a check of the accuracy of the accounting records. Goods may be valued at wholesale cost or at the retail price. Often both calculations are performed.

Wholesale Value (Cost). The cost of the same goods can vary over an accounting period and with the size of orders. Suppose 10 units of a given item were purchased in January at $100 each and 5 units were purchased in February at $125 each. What was the cost of one unit sold in March? One method is to assume that the oldest item was sold first and to price the "goods sold" at $100. This is called the **FIFO** (first in/first out) method. An alternative is to assume that the most recently purchased item (the one bought in February) was sold and to list its cost at $125. This is called the **LIFO** (last in/first out) method. In large computerized operations, merchandise may be tracked by a shipment number that permits valuing each item at its actual cost. For smaller firms, FIFO or LIFO estimates may suffice. Whichever method is being used (this may be dictated by tax considerations), the bookkeeper should use it consistently.

Retail Value.   The firm's owners may wish to know the retail value of inventory for tax reasons, for insurance purposes, or to compute the value of the business when

The most common methods for computing the wholesale value (cost) of inventory are FIFO (first in/first out) and LIFO (last in/first out).

> **The Sales Returns and Allowances account provides valuable information to management: the extent of customer dissatisfaction.**

it is sold. If the firm customarily marks up its merchandise by the same percentage over cost (say, 50%), the retail value can be computed by multiplying the wholesale value of the entire inventory by 1.5. If different items are marked up by different amounts, the only alternative may be to physically examine each price tag.

Returned Goods

Journalizing and posting of returns was already discussed in Chapter 3. When a sale is made, Sales is credited and Cash is debited. It would be simple merely to reverse this process when goods are returned, debiting Sales and crediting Cash. This may suffice in a service business where returns do not figure largely in business operations; in a merchandising operation, however, it is customary to have a ledger T account called Sales Returns and Allowances.

When a return is made, the bookkeeper *debits* the sales and allowances account and *credits* Cash or Accounts Receivable,

depending on whether the sale was a cash or a charge transaction. This method shows management the value of goods the customers were dissatisfied with. Sales returns are a "contra account" that works against the sales account and is ultimately subtracted from it.

Purchase Discounts

As already discussed in Chapter 3, purchase discounts are reductions in price that vendors offer merchandising firms for quantity orders or for prompt payment. To show discounts gained, the bookkeeper must establish a ledger T account for Purchase Discounts. When a discount is taken on a transaction, the bookkeeper *debits* Accounts Payable, *credits* Cash, and *credits* Purchase Discounts.

	Dr.	Cr.
Accounts Payable	$2,000	
Purchase Discounts		$ 200
Cash		1,800

> **The Purchase Discounts account enables management to see the monetary value of quantity purchases and prompt payment (which must be weighed against the interest that could be earned on the funds so expended).**

Finalizing the Operating Statement

Once all adjustments for inventory and returns have been made, operating expenses are entered and the operating statement is completed as it would be for a service business (**Figure 9.3**).

Figure 9.3

BETTY'S BOOTERY
Operating Statement
For the Year Ending Dec. 31, 19_____

REVENUE		
Gross Sales		$75,800
Less Sales Returns and Allowances		800
Net Sales		$75,000
COST OF GOODS SOLD		
Beginning Inventory 1/1/_____		$40,000
Purchases	$21,000	
Less Purchase Returns	1,000	
Net Purchases		$20,000
Merchandise Available for Sale		$60,000
Less Ending Inventory 12/31/_____		15,000
Cost of Goods Sold		45,000
GROSS PROFIT ON SALES		$30,000
OPERATING EXPENSES		
Rent Expense	$10,000	
Wages & Salaries Expense	10,000	
Utilities Expense	3,000	
Supplies Expense	1,000	
Advertising Expense	1,000	
Total Expenses		$25,000
NET INCOME		$ 5,000

CHAPTER TEN

Depreciation

---

accelerated depreciation
book value
depreciation
double declining balance method
fixed assets

salvage value
straight-line method
sum-of-years-digits method
units of production method

In the discussion of assets in Chapter 2, two kinds of assets were described: current assets and plant assets. Plant assets, also called **fixed assets,** include land and buildings, furniture and fixtures, vehicles, and machinery and equipment. (Together they are sometimes listed as *property, plant, and equipment*.)

What Depreciation Is

Fixed assets are not for sale; they are used in operating the business. Because they last a long time, their cost cannot logically be charged to the year in which they are purchased. But because fixed assets do wear out or become obsolete, their

> **The cost of fixed assets is spread over their useful life and charged to each year as *depreciation*.**

decline in useful value must be accounted for (and money for replacement must be budgeted). This is done by spreading their cost over their useful life and deducting a part of it each year as **depreciation** expense.

To determine the value of a piece of equipment at any time in its life, and also to determine the total current value of fixed assets when computing the balance sheet, two accounts are needed: Depreciation Expense, which becomes part of the operating expenses, and Accumulated Depreciation, which is a "contra asset" account charged against assets.

A journal entry for depreciation expense is a *debit* to the depreciation expense account and a *credit* to accumulated depreciation. Any reduction to an asset is considered an expense; however, no movement of cash or writing of a check is required for depreciation expense. The amounts must be transferred from *depreciation schedules* on which the calculations are made.

Journal

	Dr.	Cr.
Depreciation Expense	$5,000	
Accumulated Depreciation, Truck		$5,000

Although calculations of depreciation are made in terms of years, depreciation expense is deducted monthly, so the yearly figure must be divided by 12. If an asset is purchased during the first half of the month, a whole month's depreciation is customarily taken. If an item is purchased after the fifteenth of the month, depreciation might be ignored for that month and deductions begun the following month.

The **book value,** or current depreciated value of an asset (or of all assets except land), is determined by subtracting its accumulated depreciation from its cost. For example, if your firm purchased a truck for $25,000 and its accumulated depreciation was $5,000, it would appear on the Plant Assets section of the balance sheet this way:

Balance Sheet

Plant Assets		
Truck	$25,000	
Less Accumulated Depreciation	5,000	
Total Plant Assets		$20,000

If a firm owns many fixed assets, they are often grouped by category on the balance sheet, although records are maintained for the individual pieces of equipment—buildings, vehicles, office equipment, machine tools, and so on.

Land is put into a separate category because land does not depreciate.

> **Book value is the current depreciated value of a fixed asset.**

Methods of Calculating Depreciation

In figuring depreciation, several factors are taken into account:

○ The original cost of the asset
○ Its estimated useful lifetime in years
○ Its estimated **salvage value** (the trade-in value or estimated selling price at the end of its useful life)

It is not possible to determine exactly how long an asset will be useful, so some flexibility is tolerated. The IRS can provide guidelines suggesting the useful life of different kinds of equipment.

The four options in depreciation are the straight-line method, the sum-of-years-digits method, the double declining balance method, and the units of production method, which is mainly used for manufacturing equipment. The sum-of-years-digits and double declining balance methods yield **accelerated depreciation**—that is, the greatest proportion of the expense is taken in the first year, with successively smaller amounts being taken in later years. Which method is chosen is generally a management decision determined by tax or other considerations.

The Straight-Line Method

Straight-line depreciation is simplest to compute. The salvage value is deducted from the cost, and the remaining amount is divided by the estimated useful life of the asset. Suppose your firm purchased a truck that cost $25,500, was expected to last for ten years, and would be worth $500 at trade-in. Your annual depreciation would be:

$$\frac{\$25,500 - \$500}{10} = \$2,500$$

Since depreciation expense is generally charged monthly, you would divide $2,500 by 12. Each month you would *debit* depreciation expense and *credit* accumulated depreciation by $208.33 until the entire $25,000 had been accounted for.

The Sum-of-Years-Digits Method

Calculation by the **sum-of-years-digits method** employs a fraction in which the numerator consists of the remaining years of the expected lifetime and the denominator is the sum of all the years of life. For example, for an asset expected to last five years, you would add:

$$5 + 4 + 3 + 2 + 1 = 15$$

Your denominator would be 15. In the first year you would have a depreciation expense of 5/15ths of the cost (less salvage value), and so on:

5/15ths × original cost minus trade in = 1st year depreciation
4/15ths × original cost minus trade in = 2nd year depreciation
3/15ths × original cost minus trade in = 3rd year depreciation
2/15ths × original cost minus trade in = 4th year depreciation
1/15th × original cost minus trade in = 5th year depreciation
15/15ths total

The Double Declining Balance Method

Like the sum-of-years-digits method, the **double declining balance method** is an accelerated method of depreciation. In this system, residual (salvage) value is ignored until the end. The percentage of depreciation taken each year is based on the straight-line rate multiplied by two. For example, straight-line depreciation of an asset with an estimated life of four years would be 25% per year; multiplied by two this gives 50% of the asset value. That amount is deducted in the first year, and the remaining value of the asset is then multiplied by 50% to determine the second year's depreciation, and so on.

Year	Undepreciated value at beginning of year	Depreciation of 50% balance remaining
1	$25,000	$12,500
2	12,500	6,250
3	6,250	3,125
4	3,125	1,563

The final value is adjusted so that the final book value equals the residual (salvage) value that was estimated at the outset. In the foregoing example, the total depreciation taken comes to $23,438; when subtracted from $25,000 this leaves $1,562, which is considered the residual value.

Units of Production Method

Some machines become less useful as they are used. For example, the usefulness of an automobile is more a function of miles traveled than of age. The formula for the **units of production method** consists of first deducting the salvage value and then dividing the purchase price by the number of units thought to be the best indicator of usefulness (for example, mileage or hours of operation).

For example, suppose a die mold used to stamp out steel parts was estimated to be capable of stamping out 4,000 parts before becoming useless. It cost $81,000 and its salvage value is estimated to be $1,000. It stamped a total of 1,000 units in the current year, so:

$$\frac{\$81,000 - \$1,000}{\$4,000} \times 1,000 = \$20,000 \text{ (depreciation)}$$

As with the declining balance method, the final value in the above calculation would be adjusted to equal the residual value that was originally estimated.

EXERCISES

10.1 Use the straight-line method to compute the first year's depreciation and then the first monthly depreciation expense for a $3,900 computer printer with an expected life of three years and a trade-in value of $300.

10.2 Using the sum-of-the-years-digits method, calculate the depreciation for each of the three years of life of the computer printer described in Example 10.1.

10.3 Now use the double declining balance method to calculate the annual depreciation for the computer printer described in Example 10.1.

10.4 Suppose the computer printer described in the foregoing examples has an expected life of 10,000 hours and worked for 2,000 hours this year. Compute this year's depreciation.

CHAPTER ELEVEN

Checking Accounts

TERMS YOU'LL NEED TO KNOW

bank reconciliation *deposit slip* *negotiable instrument*
bank statement *drawee* *payee*
check register *drawer* *supporting document*

A **negotiable instrument** is a written promise of one person to pay a specific sum of money to another person either on demand or at a certain date in the future. The type of negotiable instrument most commonly encountered in bookkeeping is checks. Promissory notes, which are also negotiable instruments, are discussed in Chapter 13.

How Checks Are Used

A check is a written instrument that is signed by the depositor or a demand account (checking account), ordering the bank to pay a specified amount to a designated person (**Figure 11.1**). Three parties are involved:

○ The **drawer** creates the check and signs it on its *face* (the front)

○ The **payee** receives the check and must endorse (sign) it on the back to cash or deposit it.

○ The **drawee** is the bank on which the *face amount* (the sum for which the check is written) is drawn.

Business checks, available from commercial banks or specialized suppliers, are prenumbered in sequence and have stubs or vouchers on which to record the date drawn, the amount, the payee's name, and the purpose of the check.

Figure 11.1

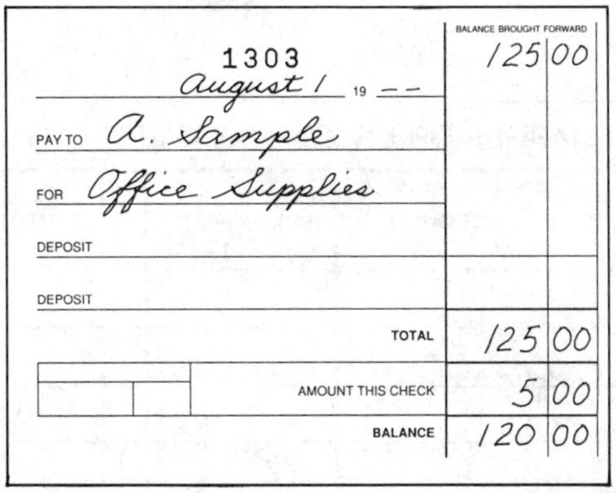

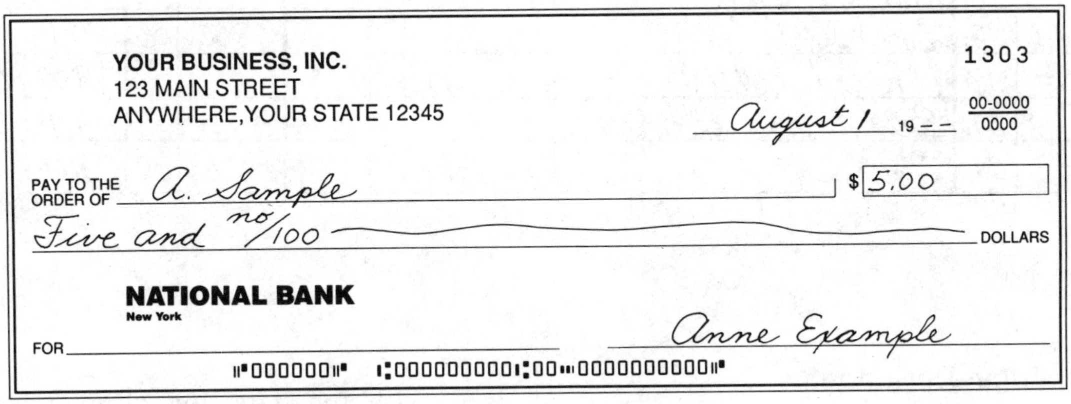

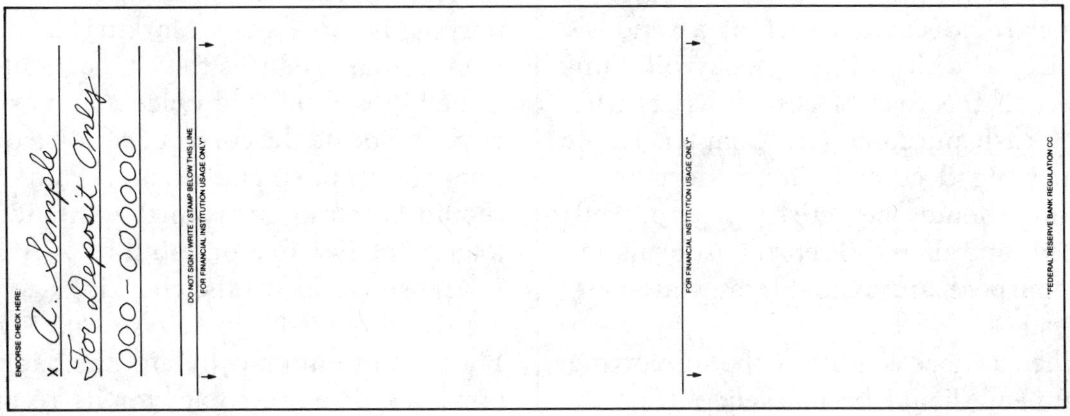

The Check Register

Some kind of running record must be kept by subtracting the amount of each check from the balance, subtracting any additional charges to the account such as bank service charges, and adding any deposit made to the account (as well as interest if the account is interest-bearing). A **check register** may be supplied for this purpose, or the check stubs may be used (**Figure 11.2**).

		RECORD ALL CHARGES OR CREDITS THAT AFFECT YOUR ACCOUNT					
NUMBER	DATE	DESCRIPTION OF TRANSACTION	(a) PAYMENT/DEBIT (−)	✓ T	FEE (IF ANY) (−)	(b) DEPOSIT/CREDIT (+)	BALANCE $ (c)
	Jan 3	Deposit	$		$	$ 1,000 00	
100	4	Ben's Trucking Co.	30 00				970 00
101	5	General Supply	100 00				870 00
102	5	A. Landlord	700 00				170 00
103	9	Juan Perez	160 00				10 00
	12	Deposit				800 00	810 00
104	13	United Federal Co.	10 00				800 00
	31	Bank service charge	7 00				793 00
	31	Interest Earned				12 00	805 00

Figure 11.2

Supporting Documents

Each check that is written requires a **supporting document** such as a vendor's invoice, a utility bill, or a payroll summary. In the case of checks written for petty cash purposes (see Chapter 12), a supporting document in the form of a memo should be created, approved, signed, and dated. (Preprinted forms for this purpose are available at stationery stores.)

When a check is written, the supporting document should be marked PAID on its face, with the date and check number noted. A rubber stamp designed for this purpose is convenient. Marking the document as paid reduces the chance that the same bill will be paid twice and makes it easier to locate the correct check if a question about payment occurs. Paid bills should be removed from the unpaid bill folder and filed in a paid-bill file.

Deposits made to the checking account are accompanied by a *deposit slip* (**Figure 11.3**). You retain a copy and the bank retains one or more copies for its records.

> Every check written should have a supporting document
> in the form of an invoice, a payroll record, or a memo.

YOUR BUSINESS, INC.
123 MAIN STREET
ANYWHERE, YOUR STATE 12345

DATE_____ 19____
CHECKS AND OTHER ITEMS ARE RECEIVED FOR DEPOSIT SUBJECT TO THE
TERMS AND CONDITIONS OF THIS INSTITUTION'S COLLECTION AGREEMENT.
DEPOSITS MAY NOT BE AVAILABLE FOR IMMEDIATE WITHDRAWAL.

CURRENCY
COIN
CHECKS
TOTAL FROM OTHER SIDE
TOTAL
Total Deposit

00-0000
0000

DEPOSIT TICKET
PLEASE ITEMIZE ADDITIONAL CHECKS ON REVERSE SIDE

PRINTER CO.

Figure 11.3

Bank Statements

At specified intervals, usually monthly, the bank will send the checking account holder a bank statement (**Figure 11.4**). This will show:

○ The depositor's beginning balance
○ Additions caused by deposits (credits)
○ Interest, if any (credits)
○ Deductions caused by checks that have been paid out by the bank (that is, checks that have "cleared")
○ Bank charges such as service charges, new checks, charges for use of automatic teller (ATM) machines.

For routine charges such as account-service charges, banks do not usually issue supporting documents, but for items such as check printing, returned-check (overdraft) charges, stop-payment charges and the like, the bank will send the depositor a debit memo.

The checks that have been received and paid by the bank (canceled checks) are returned with the statement. (These will usually not include all checks written during the statement period.) Copies of deposit slips will also be returned. The bookkeeper uses the bank statement, the canceled checks, and the deposit slips to prepare the bank reconciliation.

NATIONAL BANK
P.O. BOX 000
NEW YORK, N.Y.

PAGE 1
RELATION 1–0
41
000-0000-000

NATIONAL BANK
Member FDIC   New York

YOUR INFORMATION # 000-000-000-000   TUTOR / TAPE
107 FRANCE ST
NEW YORK N.Y.

STATEMENT FROM 07-29-90 TO 08-31-90

DESCRIPTION OF YOUR ACTIVITY	CHECKS AND OTHER CHARGES	DEPOSITS AND OTHER CREDITS	DATE	BALANCE
CHECKING ACCOUNT 000 00000				
OPENING BALANCE			07-29	2,377.97
CHECK # 815 REF 00017001762	1,000.00		08-01	1,377.97
CHECK # 816 REF 00010000539	114.00		08-02	1,263.97
CHECK # 814 REF 00015003076	30.00		08-04	
CHECK # 809 REF 00015003077	80.95		08-04	1,153.02
REGULAR DEPOSIT REF 00060000513		622.35	08-08	
CHECK # 843 REF 00013002896	1,157.19		08-24	6,230.42
CHECK # 839 REF 00013002181	12.00		08-25	
CHECK # 850 REF 00011002376	16.03		08-25	
CHECK # 851 REF 00010000487	46.16		08-25	
CHECK # 841 REF 00015001465	60.00		08-25	
CHECK # 842 REF 00010002924	673.17		08-25	
CHECK # 845 REF 00010002005	3,000.00		08-25	2,423.06
CHECK REF 00011002061	9.00		08-26	
CHECK # 838 REF 00011000108	45.00		08-26	
CHECK # 835 REF 00012000160	142.40		08-26	
CHECK # 853 REF 00018000873	180.13		08-26	2,046.53
REGULAR DEPOSIT REF 00063000069		516.80	08-29	
CHECK # 848 REF 00010001958	199.15		08-29	
CHECK # 854 REF 00011003271	993.46		08-29	1,370.72
REGULAR DEPOSIT REF 00027002834		84.99	08-30	
REGULAR DEPOSIT REF 00040002736		1,388.48	08-30	
CHECK # 856 REF 00012002161	33.90		08-30	2,810.29
CHECK # 852 REF 00027000605	10.00		08-31	
CHECK # 846 REF 00015002271	17.40		08-31	
CHECK # 819 REF 00015001778	80.00		08-31	2,702.89
ENDING BALANCE			08-31	2,702.89

Figure 11.4

Reconciling the Checking Account

As already suggested, the running balance in the check register and the final balance shown on the bank statement are not likely to agree. Some bank charges may not have been recorded (since they cannot be known until they appear on the statement), some checks may not have cleared because of delays in the reaching the bank, and some deposits may not yet have been credited. The **bank reconciliation** is prepared to verify the accuracy of the bank's records and the firm's checking account register.

Rigorous monthly reconciliation of the bank statement is critical to effective bookkeeping. Among its purposes is the prevention or discovery of embezzlement, and for this reason it is best performed by someone other than the person who issues the checks.

The steps in reconciling a bank statement are as follows:

1. Add up the amounts recorded in the past month's check stubs and compare these with the total for the month in the Cash Payments journal.

2. Sort the canceled checks into numerical order and compare each returned check with its check stub and with the bank statement. Check off the returned checks on the check register or stub and on the statement. List any that have not been returned, total them, and label this amount "checks not cleared."

3. Add up the month's deposit slips and compare the amount with (a) the total deposits recorded on the check stubs, (b) the total in the Cash Receipts journal, and (c) the total shown on the bank statement.

4. Note and add up any deposits not listed on the bank statement; label these "deposits in transit."

5. Look at the bank statement's balance of your account; *add* deposits in transit, *subtract* checks not cleared, add or subtract any bank errors, and label the resulting sum "adjusted bank balance."

6. To your check register total, *add* any additions (such as interest) made to your account by the bank; *subtract* any bank charges, add or subtract any depositor's errors, and label the resultant sum "adjusted balance."

Your adjusted balance and the adjusted bank balance should agree. If they do not, you will have to find the error and adjust your records accordingly. This work is generally done on a bank reconciliation form like the one illustrated in **Figure 11.5**.

Recording Adjustments to the Checking Account

Any adjustments made to the checking account must be entered into the check register as well as the journals. For example, if a check was recorded in an amount smaller than the face amount, the difference is a *credit* to Cash and is entered in the Cash Payments journal with an explanation. The check register must also be corrected. If the check was recorded for more than its face amount, the adjustment is

At the end of each month, a bank reconciliation must be prepared
to verify the accuracy of the check records and to make adjustments
for bank charges and any errors that have occurred.

Figure 11.5

TUTOR/TAPE CORPORATION
Bank Reconciliation
Sept. 30, 19____

Balance according to bank statement		$_____
Plus any additions or deposits not on bank statement ("in transit")	$_____	
Minus checks issued but not yet cleared by the bank ("outstanding checks")	_____	
Plus or minus any bank errors	_____	
Adjusted bank balance		$_____
Bank balance according to depositor's records		$_____
Plus any interest or additions by the bank not recorded in depositor's records	$_____	
Minus bank charges, monthly fees not recorded by depositor	_____	
Plus or minus any depositor errors	_____	
Adjusted balance		$_____

entered in brackets [$12.00] to show that this is a negative amount to be debited to the cash account.

Journal entries for bank service charges and for amounts collected by the bank are shown below.

	Dr.	Cr.
Miscellaneous Expense		
Sept. 1 Cash	$ 7.50	
Bank service charge		$ 7.50
1 Cash	800.00	
Note Receivable, Smith		800.00
Note collected by bank		

CHAPTER TWELVE

Handling Petty Cash

TERMS YOU'LL NEED TO KNOW

petty cash fund   *petty cash journal*   *petty cash voucher*

Although business payments should be made by check whenever possible, it is not always practical to do so. A check may not be acceptable in some situations (for example, for a taxi or bus fare), or no check may be available when an expenditure is made. To meet the need for small cash payments, the bookkeeper may set up a petty cash fund.

The Petty Cash Fund

To establish a **petty cash fund,** a certain sum (say, $100) is set aside for the purpose. The money may be kept in a locked petty cash box with one person being held responsible for it. No bookkeeping entry is needed when the cash is drawn, since the petty cash fund together with the cash in

Whenever cash is taken from the petty cash fund, a voucher or receipt
supporting the expenditure must be left in its place.

bank accounts equal the cash owned by the business. This kind of advance of money is called an *imprest fund;* a memorandum record of it is made, but it requires no posting to the ledger. For an active petty cash fund with frequent withdrawals, a special journal may be created (see next section).

Removals of cash from the fund must be supported by either a receipt (**Figure 12.1**) or a **petty cash voucher.** The voucher is a slip or form recording who received the money, the date, and the purpose of the expenditure; it may be signed or initialed by the person responsible for the petty cash fund. Stationers carry preprinted petty cash forms.

PETTY CASH RECEIPT

Number *24*   Date *August 10, 19--*

Paid to *Postmaster*

for *postage due*

amount *$.28*

Received payment *a. Carrier*   Approved by *R.G.*

Figure 12.1

At the end of the month, the receipts and vouchers are totaled and the remaining cash is counted. The total of receipts and vouchers plus the remaining cash must always equal the established amount.

When the cash fund runs low, it must be brought back up to the established sum.

Upon verifying the total of the receipts, the bookkeeper issues a check in that amount to the order of Petty Cash. Receipts are posted to the Cash Payments journal to *credit* cash and *debit* the appropriate expense accounts.

The Petty Cash Journal

For an active petty cash fund for which detailed or frequent records are required, a special **petty cash journal** may be set up. To open the petty cash account, a check is drawn to Petty Cash and entered in this special journal. Payments to petty cash are entered as shown in **Figure 12.2**. At the end of the month, the totals are posted as a *debit* to each individual expense account and a *credit* to Petty Cash.

19-- Date	Description	✓	Receipts	Cr. Payments	Dr. Office Exp.	Dr. Deliv. Exp.	Dr. Postage Exp.	Dr. Sales Exp.
3/1	Check No. 514	✓	$ 100.00					
3/5	Stamps	✓		$ 12 50			$ 12 50	
3/6	Oil	✓		4 10		$ 4 10		
3/12	Stationery	✓		9 40	$ 9 40			
3/15	Bulbs	✓		4 00	4 00			
3/18	Sales Luncheon	✓		24 50				24 50
3/20	Taxi	✓		8 00				8 00
3/28	Tape	✓		5 00	5 00			
				$ 67 50	$ 18 40	$ 4 10	$ 12 50	$ 32 50
				(11)	(51)	(54)	(57)	(59)
4/1	Check No. 632		$ 67.50					

Figure 12.2

Company Name
Petty Cash Journal March, 19--

CHAPTER THIRTEEN

Interest

TERMS YOU'LL NEED TO KNOW

discounted note
interest
interest rate
maturity

principal
promissory note
time

Interest is rent charged for the use of money. Most lending institution transactions involve interest in some form. Bookkeeping for businesses involves interest, too. Your firm may charge interest on past-due accounts and may hold promissory notes (signed promises to pay a certain sum by a certain date) from customers. Suppliers and creditors may charge the firm interest, and the firm may have loans or mortgages for equipment or real estate on which interest must be paid.

Interest your business pays to its creditors, including banks, is *interest expense*, and payments of interest are recorded as cash disbursements. They are a *credit* to the Cash account and a *debit* to the Interest Expense account.

Interest received from customers or debtors is *interest income*. It is a *debit* to the Cash account and a *credit* to Interest Income (Revenue).

> **Interest is rent paid for the use of money, whether you charge it to past-due creditors for the use of your money or pay it to the bank for the use of its money.**

Calculating Interest

Three elements are used in figuring the amount of interest on a borrowed sum of money.

○ The **principal** is the amount of money borrowed.
○ The **interest rate** is the amount charged for the loan, expressed as a percentage.
○ **Time** is the number of months or days the principal is held by the borrower.

The interest rate, which is stated as a yearly rate, must be adjusted to the actual length of the loan. The formula for doing this is:

$$I = PRT$$

when

I = Interest
P = Principal
R = Rate
T = Time

Interest = Principal×Rate×Time

$$\text{Interest} = \frac{\text{Principal}}{1} \times \frac{\text{Rate}}{100} \times \frac{\text{Time in Days}}{360}$$

In this formula, interest is given as a fraction with the rate as the numerator and 100 as the denominator. Most banks consider a year to consist of 360 days, not 365, for convenience in calculating; therefore in the interest equation the time is expressed as a fraction with the number of days as the numerator and 360 as the denominator. Alternatively, 12 months may be used instead of 360 days; a 3-month (90-day) loan would thus be expressed as 3/12.

For example, the interest on $1,000 ($P$) borrowed at 12% ($I$) for 60 days ($T$) is calculated as follows:

$$I = \frac{\$1,000}{1} \times \frac{12}{100} \times \frac{60}{360}$$
$$I = \$1,000 \times .12 \times .1667$$
$$I = \$20$$

Recording Interest Paid By the Business

If your firm is *paying* interest, you enter it into the Cash Payments journal in connection with the loan account. **Figure 13.1** shows such transactions. The ledger account to which the interest is eventually posted may be in the name of the holder of a mortgage, the holder of a note, or a vendor to whom a payment was made late.

Recording Interest Received By the Business

Interest is an expense when paid and a revenue when received. An Interest Income account is set up and credited whenever a payment of interest is received. This account represents an increase in capital. The transaction is entered in the cash receipts journal as a *debit* to cash and a *credit* to interest income (**Figure 13.2**).

> **The formula for calculating interest is: *I* = *PRT***

Cash Payments Journal

Ck No.	Date 19—	Payee	P/R	Explanation	Cr. Cash	Cr. Purchase Discount	Dr. Accounts Payable	Account	Dr. Account
10	June 1	State Bank		90-Day note @ 12%	$ 1010			Notes Payable	$ 1000
								Interest Expense	10
11	2	Charlo Supply		Interest on 10% note	37			Interest Expense	37
12	3	Vendall Inc.		Pay't of overdue acct.	203		$ 200	Interest Expense	3
13	5	Sharon Paper Co.		Invoice less 2%	98	$ 2	100		
					$ 1348	$ 2	$ 300		$ 1050

Figure 13.1

Cash Receipts Journal

Date 19—	Received from	P/R	Explanation	Dr. Cash	Dr. Sales Discount	Cr. Accounts Receivable	Account	Cr. Account
Jan. 2	B. Morgan		Pd. on account	$ 2000		$ 2000		
2	Smith Brothers			400		400		
2	Sales			6200			Sales	$ 6200
4	M. Hickey		Overdue acct	404		400	Interest Income	4
5	Bank		Received interest	5				5
12	S. Dove		60-day note with interest	510			Note Receivable	500
							Interest Income	10
16	Donut Ltd.		Invoice less 2%	98	$ 2	100		
17	Rick's Radiator		Interest on Mortgage	600			Interest Income	600
23	P. Sunshine		30 day note with interest	3018			Note Receivable	3000
							Interest Income	18
23	Cliff Edgcover		Overdue Acct with Interest	803		800	Interest Income	3
31	Sales			7200			Sales	7200
				$ 21238	$ 2	$ 3700		$ 17540

Figure 13.2

Handling Promissory Notes

A **promissory note** is a written commitment by one person to pay a definite sum of money to another at a specified future date. Installment loans are a form of promissory note in which payments are made periodically rather than in a lump sum. Simpler forms of promissory notes are much like checks in appearance. In current practice, however, notes and loans are more often complex documents listing not only the interest and principal but many legal conditions and terms of repayment as well. If you have taken out a car loan, for example, one of the documents you signed, the installment contract, was a form of promissory note.

When a business firm borrows money, it issues some form of promissory note as evidence of the debt. Notes for 30, 60, or 90 days (short-term borrowing) are common in business. A record of this liability and the interest expense it incurs is set up as shown below.

19—	Dr.	Cr.
June 1 Cash	$50,000	
Notes Payable		$50,000

When the note is paid, the journal entry is made like this:

	Dr.	Cr.
Sept. 1 Notes Payable	$50,000	
Interest Expense	533	
Cash		$50,533

Sometimes interest on the note is paid in advance; this kind of note is called a **discounted note.** For example, the firm borrows $5,000 for 30 days at 18% per year on a discounted note. The interest of $75 is deducted at once, and the borrower receives only $4,925 but must pay back $5,000 at **maturity,** the date when the loan comes due (in this case, at the end of 30 days).

In the transaction shown below, 10,000 was borrowed on June 1 in the form of a 90-day discounted note on which the interest was $1,000:

	Dr.	Cr.
June 1 Cash	$9,000	
Interest Expense	1,000	
Notes Payable		$10,000

When the note matures on September 1 and is paid, the entry would look like this:

	Dr.	Cr.
Sept. 1 Notes Payable	$10,000	
Cash		$10,000

Sometimes—for example, in the purchase of vehicles or equipment—a cash down payment is made, leaving a sum to be paid off. A note is signed for this balance. Suppose your firm purchases a machine costing $35,000, making a down payment of $5,000 and signing a note for $30,000:

	Dr.	Cr.
Feb. 2 Machinery	$35,000	
Cash		$ 5,000
Notes Payable		30,000

When part of this note is paid, the principal is recorded to Notes Payable and the interest to Interest Expense:

	Dr.	Cr.
Mar. 2 Notes Payable	$5,000	
Interest Expense	75	
Cash		$5,075

EXERCISES

13.1 Using the work sheet provided, enter the following transactions into the Cash Payments journal. Indicate the accounts to which postings would be made, but do not post.

June 1: Sent check of $303 to A. North to pay 60-day note of $300 plus interest of $3.00.

June 5: Sent check of $277.75 to Gibson Company for past due account of $275 plus interest of $2.75.

June 8: Sent check of $6,000 to Stern Company for semiannual interest due on mortgage of $100,000 at rate of 12% per year.

June 12: Paid note of $5,000 owed to City Banks with interest of 10% for 2 months ($I = PRT = \$83.33$).

June 15: Paid $360 to Arless Company for overdue account plus 6% interest at $1.80.

June 21: Sent check of $9,000 to Tryson Mortgage Company for quarterly interest due on mortgage of $400,000 at a rate of 9% per year ($I = PRT = \$9,000$).

Cash Payments Journal, June, 19__

Ck No.	Date	Payee	P/R	Explanation	Cr. Cash	Cr. Purchase Discount	Dr. Accounts Payable	Account	Dr. Amount
1									
2									
3									
4									
5									
6									
7									
8									
9									
10									
11									
12									
13									
14									
15									
16									
17									
18									
19									
20									
21									
22									
23									
24									

13.2 Using the work sheet provided, enter the following into the Cash Receipts journal and show where the entries would be posted.

Mar. 5: Received check for $303 from L. Herbit on his overdue account of $300 plus $3.00 interest.

Mar. 8: Bank credited your firm's account with $3.00 interest on one of your accounts.

Mar. 12: L. Crane sent check for $606 for his 60-day note with principal of $600 and interest of $6.00.

Mar. 13: Received check from R. Ralston in payment of invoice of $450 less a 2% discount.

Mar. 15: Received check for $500 from Richards & Company in payment of monthly interest on their mortgage.

Mar. 18: Received check for $3,015 from L. Johnson for her 30-day note of $3,000 and interest.

Mar. 25: John Good paid his overdue account of $400 plus interest of $2.00.

Cash Receipts Journal

Date	Received from	P/R	Explanation	Dr. Cash	Cr. Sales Discount	Cr. Accounts Receivable	Account	Cr. Amount

CHAPTER FOURTEEN

Payroll Records

TERMS YOU'LL NEED TO KNOW

FICA

Form W-2

gross wages

individual earnings record

individual payroll report

net wages

payroll deductions

payroll register

salaries

wages

Payroll records keep track of wages and salaries. **Wages** are hourly compensation for nonmanagement employees; **salaries** are compensation paid to supervisory and management employees who are hired at a flat yearly, monthly, or (sometimes) weekly compensation.

Keeping Hourly Records and Computing Wages

The hours worked by salaried employees are not normally recorded. For wage earners, however, records of hours must be kept not only to compute their compensation but to comply with local, state, and federal wage and hour laws and (in some cases) union regulations. For example, most states and the federal government require that time and a half be paid to employees who work more than 40 hours in a week. Some employee contracts specify that double the usual hourly rate be paid for work done on Sundays or holidays, and some employers pay a premium for evening or night shift work.

The term *gross wages* refers to the employee's compensation for the pay period before the deduction of taxes or any benefits paid for by the employee.

A time clock or an in/out log may be used to keep workers' hours. Regular wages are computed by multiplying the hourly rate by the hours worked; overtime is usually computed separately. The worker's regular wages ("straight time") plus overtime, if any, are called **gross wages.**

For salaried personnel, the gross wages for the pay period consist of the annual salary divided by the number of pay periods in the working year. (For example, a salaried worker earning $24,000 a year and paid monthly would have a gross wage of $2,000 for the pay period.)

In some types of businesses, such as automobile sales or real estate, sales personnel are paid commissions as all or part of their compensation. Computation of commission is not addressed here; however, the computation of deductions from wages would be the same as described here.

Payroll Deductions

All business firms with employees are required by law to deduct certain state, federal, and (sometimes) local taxes and to remit these taxes directly to the government. Union dues may have to be deducted and accounted for. In addition, deductions may be made for insurance and other items for which the employee pays in whole or in part. The amount remaining after all deductions is called **net wages.**

Taxes Withheld From the Employee

Federal and state income taxes and local wage taxes (if any) are withheld from the employee's pay and remitted directly to the appropriate government agency.

Federal Wage Tax and Social Security (FICA)

On printed payroll forms, federal income tax appears as FWT (federal wage tax). What is more commonly called "social security" appears as **FICA** (Federal Insurance Contributions Act). The employer must contribute an equal amount to the FICA; this is discussed under Taxes Paid by the Employer. The rates for tax withholdings and employer contributions change yearly. The Internal Revenue Service (IRS) can supply the current rates.

State and Local Income and Wage Taxes

State and local income taxes are similarly deducted from the employee's pay. If the appropriate rate schedules and forms are not available, the employer must secure them.

Unemployment and Disability Taxes

In some states, a portion of the unemployment tax must be withheld from employees. In other states, unemployment taxes are solely the responsibility of the employer. The same is true of state disability funds.

Taxes and Benefits Paid By the Employer

As already stated, employers must contribute an equal percentage of their employees' FICA (social security) taxes—that is, if the current withholding rate is 7.0% the employer must remit an additional 7.0% for a total of 14% of employee wages and salaries. Employers must pay state unemployment taxes in whole or in part, depending on the state, and they are liable for federal unemployment taxes if they employ more than a specified number of people. Workers' compensation insurance must also be paid on the basis of payroll, either to the state or to a private insurer, depending on state regulations.

In addition, health and dental insurance and other fringe benefits may be payroll-related, with or without the employees' contributing from their pay.

Reporting Wages and Tax Withholding

Federal taxes withheld from employees must be reported at least quarterly; firms with large numbers of employees may be required to report monthly or even weekly. Checks for the amounts withheld plus employer contributions are drawn and sent at that time. In January, employees receive **Form W-2** showing their wages and withholdings for the preceding calendar year.

State and local reporting requirements vary; however, copies of Form W-2 are sent to state taxing agencies in state that have an income tax.

Maintaining Payroll Records

The Individual Earnings Record

An **individual earnings record** is established for each employee. This record facilitates the completion of quarterly and annual reports to various taxing agencies. It enables the employer to send out **Form W-2**s at year-end to all persons employed during the year. This form states the employee's wages and the FWT, FICA, and state income taxes withheld; it must be filed with an individual's income tax return. **Figure 14.1** shows a typical individual earnings record form.

Federal, state, and local tax rates and reporting regulations are constantly changing; the firm's owners or the bookkeeper should make sure that the appropriate agencies are contacted for information before payroll procedures are set up.

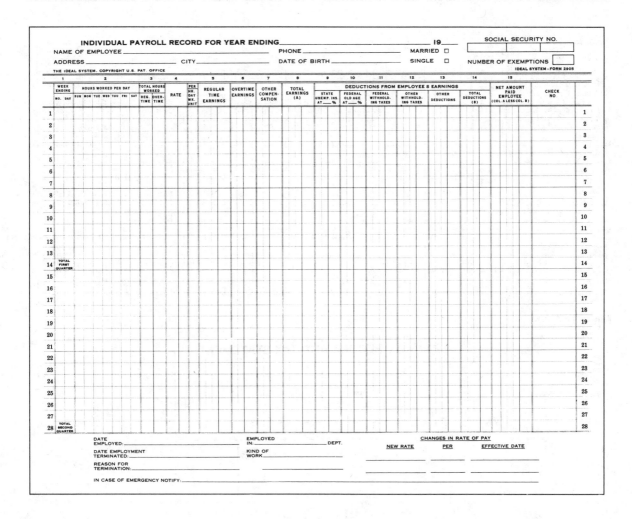

Figure 14.1

The Payroll Register

In addition to individual records, a **payroll register** for the entire firm is prepared for each payroll period, sometimes weekly (**Figure 14.2**). This register lists the names of employees, their hours worked, straight and overtime pay, gross pay, itemized deductions, and net pay. The individual columns are totaled and used to prepare journal entries. The total of the Net Pay column should equal the total of all paychecks for that period.

The Employee's Individual Payroll Report

With each paycheck, the employee receives a form showing gross earnings for the pay period, itemizing amounts withheld and showing net wages (**Figure 14.3**). Printed forms for this purpose can be purchased from a stationer. Voucher-style checks incorporating payroll information may also be purchased.

WEEK ENDING _____ January 31, _____ 19 _ _

NAME	Exemptions	SUN.	MON.	TUES.	WED.	THURS.	FRI.	SAT.	TOTAL HOURS	RATE	REGULAR	OVERTIME	OTHER	TOTAL WAGES	SOC. SEC.	U.S. WITH. TAX	STATE WITH. TAX	NET PAY	TOTAL WAGES	SOC. SEC.	U.S. WITH. TAX	STATE WITH. TAX	
Cynthia Yost	S 1								38	5.00	190 -			190 -	11 65	27 -	5 45	145 90	760 -	46 60	108 -	21 80	1
Deborah Kerr	S 2								44	5.00	200 -	30 -		220 -	14 40	31 40	6 70	171 80	920 -	56 40	125 60	26 80	2
Anna L Winson	S 2								40	5.00	200 -			200 -	12 26	25 10	5 25	157 39	800 -	49 04	100 40	21 -	3
Nancy O Daley	M 2								43	5.60	224 -	25 20		249 20	15 28	26 40	5 35	202 17	996 80	61 12	105 60	21 40	4
Glen E Baldoni	S 1								30	5.60	168 -			168 -	10 30	20 70	4 10	132 90	672 -	41 20	82 80	16 40	5
Joseph E DeCesare	M 3								35	5.80	203 -			203 -	12 44	15 80	3 40	171 36	812 -	49 76	63 20	13 60	6
Nicholas Vassar	S 1								42	5.00	200 -	15 -		215 -	13 18	31 20	6 40	164 22	860 -	52 72	124 80	25 60	7

Figure 14.2

PAYROLL RECORD AND TAX STATEMENT

Date Paid _____ 19 _____

Employer's Name _____

Employee's Name _____

Employee's Number _____ Nature of Work _____

Wages of Salary from	to	19	TOTAL HOURS	RATE PER HR	AMOUNTS
Hours Regular	SUN. MON. TUES. WED. THUR. FRI. SAT.				
Hours Overtime					

NON-CASH COMPENSATION (Meals, Room, Etc.) DESCRIBE   (A)

OTHER CASH COMPENSATION (Commissions Etc.) DESCRIBE

TOTAL WAGES   (or Salary if on Weekly, Semi-Monthly or Monthly Basis)

TIPS REPORTED RECEIVED BY EMPLOYEE   (B)

TOTAL EARNINGS — Including Tips

TAX DEDUCTIONS

___ % F.I.C.A.

___ % FEDERAL WITHHOLDING TAX

___ % S.D.I.

___ % STATE WITHHOLDING TAX (If Any)

___ % CITY WITHHOLDING TAX (If Any)

LESS: TOTAL TAX DEDUCTIONS

NET EARNINGS AFTER TAX DEDUCTIONS

OTHER DEDUCTIONS

NON-CASH COMPENSATION   (Line A Above)

TIPS REPORTED RECEIVED BY EMPLOYEE   (Line B Above)

OTHER (Describe)

OTHER (Describe)

LESS: TOTAL OTHER DEDUCTIONS

PAID IN CASH ☐   PAID BY CHECK NO. ☐   NET AMOUNT PAID EMPLOYEE

I Acknowledge Receipt and Correctness of the Above

SIGNED _____ (Employee)

Yellow Copy Employer   White Copy Employee

MADE IN U.S.A.   IDEAL SYSTEM FORM 917

Figure 14.3

Entering Payroll Information on the Books

Gross pay must be recognized as a business expense. The following journal entries are made as required, with the payroll register as the source of the information.

	Dr.	Cr.
Debit Office Salaries Expense	xx	
Debit Sales Salaries Expense	xx	
Debit Administrative Salaries Expense	xx	
Debit Wage Expense	xx	

The amounts withheld are credited to the appropriate accounts to establish them as liabilities. When these moneys are paid out, the appropriate accounts are debited.

	Dr.	Cr.
Credit FICA Payable		xx
Credit Federal Income Tax Payable		xx
Credit State Income Tax Payable		xx
Credit Union Dues Payable		xx
Credit Salaries Payable (Net Amt.)		xx

Payroll-related taxes are journalized in the following manner:

	Dr.	Cr.
Debit Payroll Tax Expense	xx	
Credit FICA Taxes Payable		xx
Credit State Unemployment Taxes Payable		xx
Credit Federal Unemployment Taxes Payable		xx

Additional accounts for such items as payroll-related insurance may be needed as well. These deductions vary too widely to be discussed here.

When all these records are complete, payroll checks may be written or printed. Today, many firms hire services that use computers to make out checks and maintain payroll records. For those who do not, individual computer programs are available that calculate taxes and debit and credit the appropriate account, as well as print out checks (see Chapter 17, "Bookkeeping and the Computer").

CHAPTER FIFTEEN

Partnerships

TERMS YOU'LL NEED TO KNOW

goodwill   *partnership*

Throughout this book, bookkeeping has been discussed in terms of a proprietorship, a one-owner business in which all profits go to a single individual and only one drawing account is used. A **partnership** is a form of business in which two or more persons invest their capital, undertaking a "joint and several" liability (risk) and sharing the profits.

Most bookkeeping for a partnership is like that for a sole proprietorship. However, two or more capital accounts must be set up to show the ownership equity of each partner, arrangements must be made to distribute the profits, and provision may have to be made for additional partners to join the business.

Capital Accounts

With two persons in the partnership, two capital accounts would be set up in the ledger: for example, "John Smith,

Capital" and "Mary Jones, Capital." Similar accounts would be set up for new partners entering the business. The opening entries for each partner would show the amount invested in the business. As the partnership expands, new capital accounts are set up showing the investment of new partners.

Transfers of Interest

When a new partner buys into a firm, one or all of the existing partners might sell the newcomer a portion of their interest in the business. In this case, the seller of an interest keeps the money paid for it, and the capital of the business remains the same as before. An entry might be made in the books to record the transfer of interest: The journal entry might read: "M. Jones sold J. Brown half interest in the business for $125,000." A *debit* in this amount would be posted to the general account. The entry to record the new partner's interest might read: "J. Brown received half interest in M. Jones's capital." A *credit* of $250,000 would be posted to the general account.

Goodwill

As a business establishes a reputation in the community for reliability and good service, an intangible asset called **goodwill** is created. This value is addition to the tangible assets such as land, equipment, or fixtures. When a new partner enters the business, he or she may be charged a price for this goodwill. A mem-

orandum journal entry might *debit* Cash and *credit* existing partners' capital accounts: "To credit M. Jones with goodwill upon admission of J. Brown as partner." The journal entry would look like this:

		Dr.	Cr.
Sept. 1	Cash	$100,000	
	Goodwill	25,000	
	M. Jones, Capital		$125,000

Drawing Accounts

If it is agreed that the partners will draw a salary, this withdrawal of cash would be treated as an operating expense to the business and would *debit* Salary Expense. Other removal of cash for personal use would be shown as a *credit* to the cash account and a *debit* to the partner's drawing account, just as it would for a proprietorship. Drawing accounts are discussed in Chapter 8.

Distributing Partnership Profits

Sometimes profits are distributed equally between or among partners; they are simply divided by the number of partners. Sometimes the partnership agreement calls for distribution of profits in proportion to each partner's investment. Suppose Smith invested $250,000, Jones invested $250,000, and Brown invested $125,000. Smith and Jones would each receive 250/625 (40%) of the profits and Brown would receive 125/625 (20%).

The Balance Sheet for a Partnership

The balance sheet for a partnership resembles that for a proprietorship. The only difference is that in the Capital section, each owner's equity (capital) is shown separately:

Balance Sheet

CAPITAL

J. Smith, Capital	$250,000	
M. Jones, Capital	250,000	
J. Brown, Capital	125,000	
Total Capital:		$625,000

Corporations

In the United States, the corporation is the second most popular form of business ownership. The proprietorship is first, and partnerships are third.

What a Corporation Is

A **corporation** is a legal entity created to separate the assets and liabilities of the business from the personal assets and liabilities of its owners. Business corporations are formed for profit, although nonprofit corporations also exist for charitable, religious, and philanthropic endeavors.

The owners of a corporation are called *shareholders* or *stockholders*, because their ownership takes the form of shares of stock. A corporation may be owned by a family, by a few individuals, or by members of the general public. The portion of the corporation's profits that is paid out to stockholders is called **dividends;** any part that is kept and reinvested in the business is called **retained earnings.**

Stock may be issued to start the business or later, to raise additional money for expansion or other purposes. It is issued in the form of certificates which may, if the corporation is publicly held, be sold and resold by their owners or those representing them. The face value of a stock certificate—that is, the price for which it was issued to its original purchasers—is called its **par value** or simply "par."

As a legal entity, a corporation can do anything an individual owner could do: own property, buy, sell, manufacture, be a party to contracts, sue or be sued, and be taxed.

Corporate bookkeeping may be extremely complex and must be performed or at least reviewed by Certified Public Accountants. Corporations that sell their stock to the public are subject to many state and federal laws. No attempt is made here to describe the complexities of corporate bookkeeping; however, it is useful for bookkeepers to know at least the types of stock that corporations issue.

Types of Corporate Stock

A number of kinds of stock may be issued. A major difference among types of stock is whether or not they convey voting rights—that is, a say in how the business is run—to their owners.

○ *Common stock* carries voting rights, and its owners share equally in any dividends that are distributed.
○ Owners of *preferred stock* receive their dividends first if the corporation does not earn enough money to pay dividends to all stockholders.

○ Holders of *preferred participating stock* enjoy the possibility of receiving dividends in excess of a specified amount.
○ For holders of *preferred nonparticipating stock*, dividends are limited to a specified amount.
○ Holders of *cumulative preferred stock* receive payment for any prior years' dividends that were missed before other stockholders receive their payments. Preferred stock that does not carry this privilege is called *noncumulative preferred stock*.

Treasury Stock

On occasion a corporation may repurchase (buy back) stock that it had previously issued. The holding of a firm's own stock is called **treasury stock.** A company is not permitted to own part of itself, and treasury stock carries no voting rights or dividends. Treasury stock is not an asset; it is a reduction of outstanding shares of the corporation's stock.

Equity Per Share

One item on the balance sheet or annual report of a corporation of concern to stockholders is the **equity per share.** This is not the par value of the stock or its value in the stock market. Instead, the equity per share represents the owners' equity, or capital value, or the business divided by the number of shares outstanding. Thus, if the owners' equity were $500,000 and 50,000 shares of stock were outstanding, the equity per share would be $500,000/$50,000 or $10 a share.

CHAPTER SEVENTEEN

Bookkeeping and the Computer

TERMS YOU'LL NEED TO KNOW

hardware   *software*   *spreadsheet program*

As computers become less expensive, more powerful, and easier to use, they are taking over some of the more tedious tasks of the bookkeeper in even the smallest businesses. A vast variety of **software** (see page 114: A Mini-Glossary of Computer Terms) is available to handle bookkeeping tasks. Some software programs are designed for small "one-person shops," others for larger firms, and many for specialized types of businesses such as law and contracting firms.

Computer technology changes so fast that even magazines find it difficult to keep up; therefore it is not practical to give precise instructions for computer bookkeeping in a book. Instead, this chapter gives an overview of the capabilities of certain types of programs and a brief introduction to how they are used. *Small Business Made Simple*, a companion volume in this series, contains a chapter on the use of computers in business that you may find it helpful to consult.

A MINI-GLOSSARY OF COMPUTER TERMS

○ **PCs** Microcomputers of the kind used by most small businesses; term comes from "personal computer."

○ **RAM** Random Access Memory. A measure of the amount of data a computer can address at any one time. Stated in kilobytes, as 640K, or megabytes, as 1.2M

○ **ROM** Read Only Memory. The internal "memory" by which the computer runs itself; of no direct importance to the user.

○ **hardware** The equipment itself— central processing unit (CPU), monitor, keyboard, disk drives.

○ **DOS** Disk operating system by which the computer "reads" and "writes" data to work with it and to store it permanently.

○ **floppies** Magnetized plastic disks, most commonly 5″ or 3.5″ round, on which data and programs are stored.

○ **software** The "programs" through which the computer actually operates. Virtually all programs used in business are purchased rather than being created by the user.

○ **spreadsheet** A program that permits the user to enter and manipulate many columns of data by equations set up by the user (see text).

NOTE: For a more complete description of PCs and how they are used in business, see Gallagher: *Your Small Business Made Simple* (Doubleday, 1989).

Capabilities of the Computer

A computer can speed up many bookkeeping operations once a program has been set up with the basic accounts. Its calculations will be only as accurate as the information its human operator provides, however.

When combined with a printer, a computer with graphics capabilities can turn profit and loss information and business plans into charts and graphs. It can instantly update inventory or accounts payable, print checks while automatically updating the appropriate accounts, put information into alphabetical, chronological, or numerical sequence, calculate interest or compare payment terms at different interest rates of maturities, and many similar tasks.

Suppose you wanted to compare the effect of depreciation on profits and taxes using the sum-of-the-years-digits method versus the straight-line method. By changing a few figures you could have the result instantly, on the screen or printed out. With a *modem*, a device that permits the computer to transmit information via telephone lines, you can send information to another location.

In your most important bookkeeping responsibilities—preparation of the financial statements used in planning budgeting and planning—a type of program called a spreadsheet can be invaluable.

Information produced by a computer is only as accurate as the information provided to the computer by its human operator, a fact reflected by the acronym GIGO (garbage in/garbage out).

Spreadsheet Programs

A **spreadsheet program** is designed to manipulate data entered into rows and columns. One of the earliest spreadsheet programs, VisiCalc®, greatly speeded up bookkeeping operations. At present, Lotus 1-2-3® is the most widely used spreadsheet. These programs are continually being updated by their manufacturers, with more and more features being added to create "integrated software" that incorporates word processing and the management of data bases that facilitate keeping and updating inventories of goods for sale and supplies.

With a spreadsheet program, the "framework" of rows and columns appears on the screen. Individual locations in the rows and columns are called *cells*. Columns run from top to bottom and may be labeled A, B, C, and so on. Rows run from left to right and may be labeled 1, 2, 3, and so on. (See **Figure 17.1**). You may label columns to store words, some to store numerical entries, some to store results of calculations. The columns can be totaled as needed, for example to show quarterly or yearly totals. Rows may also be totaled and subtotaled. Various rows and columns may be multiplied, divided, and otherwise manipulated as required by the function you are performing.

Figure 17.1

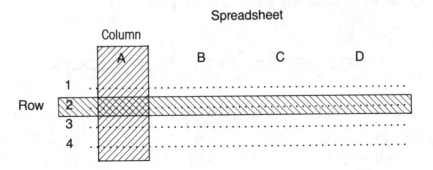

Spreadsheet

To use the program you begin by "defining," or labeling, the rows and columns. Then you instruct the computer regarding what calculation or equation it is to perform with the rows and columns. For example, you may tell it that the data in Row 1 should be added by the formula d1 = a1 + b1 + c1. Or that Column 5 should be added by the formula 5a = 1a + 2a + 3a + 4a.

The formula used to manipulate spreadsheet entries can be stored and used whenever a similar calculation must be performed.

These formulas can be permanently stored so that the program will use them each time.

Your next step is to enter the appropriate data into the individual cells. To do this, you move the *cursor* (the blinking symbol that tells you "where the computer is" in the data) to the appropriate cell and type in the information. **Figure 17.2** shows a simple setup that will compute operating expenses by type (the rows) and period incurred (the columns).

Figure 17.2

		COLUMN 1	COLUMN 2	COLUMN 3	COLUMN 4
1	ELECTRIC(A)	$ 6	$ 5	$ 5	$16
2	GAS	4(B)	4	3	11
3	WATER	2	2	1	5
4	TELEPHONE	7	6	7	20
5	TOTAL	19(C)	17	16	52

You can also set up a spreadsheet to show the income from different jobs or projects during specified periods of time (**Figure 17.3**).

Figure 17.3

MAPLE TREE COMPANY INCOME SPREADSHEET

INCOME	JAN	FEB	MAR	TOTAL	APR	MAY	JUN	TOTAL
JOB 1	50	50	50	150	50	50	50	300
JOB 2	40	40	40	120	40	40	40	240
JOB 3	60	30	50	140	20	20	10	190
TOTALS	150	120	140	410	110	110	100	730

These are very simple examples. A more complex spreadsheet might show depreciation schedules for hundreds of items of equipment. Or it might contain current and projected operating statements, with each item on the statement (revenues, cost of goods sold, individual operating expenses, gross and net profits) in a column and the years of operation in rows. By changing a single figure—say, by increasing revenue by 20% or taxes by 50%—you could project the effect on net income or profit for the current year and all ensuing years. You can then print out this information for comparison with a different projection.

Complex spreadsheets with many columns cannot be viewed on the screen all at once. However, they may be "scrolled" sideways or up and down on the screen. Some programs offer "windows" by which a chosen portion of the spreadsheet may be superimposed on a part of the screen.

Spreadsheet programs are complex and sometimes difficult to learn. Once mastered, however, they more than repay the effort involved. Computer vendors generally offer a certain amount of training with the purchase price, and community colleges and private institutions offer courses on the more popular programs.

SOLUTIONS

Exercise 2.1

JONES CO.
Balance Sheet
June 30, 19____

ASSETS			LIABILITIES		
CURRENT ASSETS			CURRENT LIABILITIES		
Cash	$ 600		Accounts Payable	$ 300	
Accounts Receivable	2,500		Bank Note	1,200	
Merchandise	1,000		Total Cur. Liabilities		$1,500
Prepaid Rent	2,000				
Total Current Assets		$6,100	LONG-TERM LIABILITIES		
			Note Payable	$6,000	
PLANT ASSETS			Total Long-Term Liabilities		$6,000
Typewriter	$ 900		Total Liabilities		$7,500
Store Equipment	1,400				
Total Plant Assets		$2,300	CAPITAL		
			Owner's Equity		$ 900
TOTAL ASSETS		$8,400	TOTAL LIABILITIES AND CAPITAL		$8,400

Exercise 2.2

1. asset
2. liability
3. capital
4. liability
5. asset
6. asset
7. asset
8. liability

Exercise 2.3

AMY'S BEAUTY SHOPPE
Operating Statement
for 3 months ended March 31, 19____

REVENUES		
Sales	$25,000	
Service	50,000	
Total Revenues		$75,000
EXPENSES		
Wages	$ 23,000	
Rent	6,000	
Electric	1,000	
Insurance	900	
Total Expenses		$30,900
NET INCOME		$44,100

Exercise 3.1

Young Company
General Journal

19--		Dr.	Cr.
Jan 2	Cash	$ 10000	
	J. Young, Capital		$ 10000
	Owner invests cash		
	into business		
3	Rent Expense	1000	
	Cash		1000
	Paid January, 19--, Rent		
5	Supplies	50	
	Cash		50
	Purchased Office Supplies		
9	Inventory	900	
	Accounts Payable		900
	Purchased Inventory		
	on Account		
14	Cash	250	
	Sales Revenue		250
	Sales for Week of 1-14		
29	Owner's Drawing Account	500	
	Cash		500
	Owner Withdraws		
	Cash		

Exercise 3.2

General Journal

19--		1 Dr.	2 Cr.
Feb 12	Rent Expense	$ 1000	
	Cash		$ 1000
	Paid Feb 19 - Rent		
12	Wages Expense	2000	
	Cash		2000
	Paid Wages Week		
	of Feb 12.		
12	Insurance Expense	800	
	Cash		800
	Paid Fire Insurance		
	Policy		

Exercise 4.1

Date	P/R	Cash Acct. #10 Dr.	Cr.
Apr. 2	J7	$ 3000	
3	J7		$ 900
9	J7	3300	
15	J7		1400
30	J7		500
Balance		$ 3500	

Date	P/R	Accounts Payable #21 Jay Co. Dr.	Cr.
Apr. 4	J7		$ 500
30	J7	$ 500	
Balance			– 0 –

Date	P/R	Supplies on Hand #12 Dr.	Cr.
Apr. 4	J7	$ 500	
Balance		$ 500	

Date	P/R	Sales Revenue #41 Dr.	Cr.
Apr. 2	J7		$ 3000
9	J7		3300
Balance			$ 6300

Date	P/R	Advertising Exp. #56 Dr.	Cr.
Apr. 3	J7	$ 900	
Balance		$ 900	

Date	P/R	Wages Exp. #52 Dr.	Cr.
Apr. 15	J7	$ 1400	
Balance		$ 1400	

Exercise 4.2

	Notes Payable # 21	Dr.	Cr.
1		$ — 0 —	$ 9000
2		1000	— 0 —
3		1000	— 0 —
4		1000	— 0 —
5	Account Balance		$ 6000
6			
7			
8			
9			
10			

Exercise 4.3

Trial Balance, April 30, 19__

	Acct. No.		Dr.	Cr.
1	10	Cash	$ 3500	
2	12	Supplies	500	
3	41	Sales Revenue		$ 6300
4	21	Accts. Payable-Jay Co.		—
5	56	Advertising Expense	900	
6	58	Wages Expense	1400	
7			$ 6300	$ 6300
8				

Exercise 5.1

Cash Receipts Journal

Date 19--	Acct. Cr.	Post Ref.	Sundry Acct. Cr. (1)	Sales Cr. (2)	Accts. Rec. Cr. (3)	Sales Disc. Dr. (4)	Cash Dr. (5)
Aug. 1	R. Brown				$ 2000		$ 2000
1	Blue + Sons				500	$ 10	490
1	Sales			$ 1600			$ 1600
2	S. Hamilton				1000	100	900
2	Cash Service Revenue		$ 750				750
3	T. Gallagher				90		90
			$ 750	$ 1600	$ 3590	$ 110	$ 5830
				$ 5940		$ 5940	

Exercise 5.2

Cash Payments Journal

Date	Ck. No.	Acct. Dr.	Post Ref.	Sundry Acct. Dr.	Accts. Pay. Dr.	Purch. Disc. Cr.	Cash Cr.
19-- Sept. 1	1	Purchases		$ 1200			$ 1200
1	2	Volt Electric Co.	✓		$ 1000	$ 20	980
2	3	Salaries Expense		800			800
3	4	Winston Bros.	✓		600	60	540
5	5	Purchases		200		50	150
6	6	Advertising Expense		95			95

Purchases Journal

Date	Acct. Credited	Post Ref.	Acct. Pay. Cr.	Purchases Dr.	Store Supplies Dr.	Office Supplies Dr.	Sundry Acct. Dr.
19-- Sept. 2	A-V. Tronics	✓	$ 3000	$ 3000			

Sales Journal

Date	Inv. No.	Acct. Dr.	Post Ref.	Accounts Receivable Dr. Sales Cr.
19-- Sept. 3		Ramco	✓	$ 9000
4		Sales	✓	370
7		Office Equipt.	✓	50

Exercise 6.1

Select Sheet Co.
Work Sheet
June 30, 19—

Acct. No.	Account	Unadjusted Trial Balance Dr.	Unadjusted Trial Balance Cr.	Adjustments Dr.	Adjustments Cr.	Adjusted Trial Balance Dr.	Adjusted Trial Balance Cr.	Income Statement Dr.	Income Statement Cr.	Balance Sheet Dr.	Balance Sheet Cr.
10	Cash	$ 3000				$ 3000				$ 3000	
11	Accounts Receivable	2000				2000				2000	
12	Office Supplies	2400			(a)$ 2000	400				400	
13	Prepaid Rent	1200			(b) 1200						
14	Tools & Equip.	1000				1000				1000	
15	Accum. Deprec.		$ 500		(c) 400		$ 900				$ 900
21	Accts. Payable		800				800				800
31	G. Trout, Capital		6500				6500				6500
32	G. Trout, Drawing	3000				3000				3000	
40	Sales		16000				16000		$ 16000		
51	Salary Expense	11000		(d)$ 1000		12000		$ 12000			
53	Misc. Expenses	200				200		200			
		$ 23800	$ 23800								
55	Office Supplies Expense			(a) 2000		2000		2000			
58	Rent Expense			(b) 1200		1200		1200			
59	Depreciation Expense			(c) 400		400		400			
24	Salaries Payable				(d) 1000		1000				1000
				$ 4600	$ 4600	$ 25200	$ 25200	$ 15800	$ 16000	$ 9400	$ 9200
	Net Income (Loss)							200			200
								$ 16000	$ 16000	$ 9400	$ 9400

Select Sheet Co.
General Journal

	19__	P/R	Dr.	Cr.	
1	Adjusting Entries				
2	Jun. 30 Office Supplies Expense		$ 2000		
3	Office Supplies			$ 2000	
4					
5	30 Rent Expense		1200		
6	Prepaid Rent			1200	
7					
8	30 Depreciation Expense		400		
9	Accumulated Depreciation			400	
10					
11	30 Salaries Expense		1000		
12	Salaries Payable			1000	
13					

Select Sheet Co.
OPERATING STATEMENT
Year ended June 30, 19--

		1	2	3	4	5	
1	Income						1
2	Sales Revenue		$ 16000				2
3	Total Revenue			$ 16000			3
4							4
5	Expenses						5
6	Salary		$ 12000				6
7	Office Supplies		2000				7
8	Rent		1200				8
9	Depreciation		400				9
10	Miscellaneous		200				10
11	Total Expenses			$ 15800			11
12	Net Income			$ 200			12
13							13
14							14
15							15
16							16
17							17
18							18

Exercise 7.1a

Exercise 7.1b

			Select Sheet Co.				
			Balance Sheet				
			June 30, 19__				

	ASSETS			LIABILITIES			
Current Assets				Current Liabilities			
Cash	$ 3000			Salaries Payable $ 1000			
Accounts Receivable	2000			Accounts Payable 800			
Office Supplies	400						
Total Curr. Assets		$ 5400		Total Curr. Liabilities		$ 1800	
Plant Assets				CAPITAL			
Tools & Equipt.	1000			J. Trout, Capital		3700	
Less Accumulated Depreciation	900						
		$ 100					
Total Assets		$ 5500		Total Liabilities + Capital		$ 5500	

Exercise 10.1

$$\frac{\text{Cost} - \text{Residual Value}}{\text{Life}} = \text{Annual Depreciation}$$

$$\frac{\$3,900 - \$300}{3} = \quad " \qquad "$$

$$\frac{\$3,600}{3} = \quad " \qquad "$$

$$\$1,200 = \quad " \qquad "$$

$$\frac{\$1,200}{12 \text{ months}} = \underline{\$100} \text{ Monthly Depreciation}$$

Exercise 10.2

3+2+1=6, The Fraction's Denominator

$$\text{Cost}-\text{Residual Value} \times \frac{\text{Rate}}{\text{Sum of the Years}}$$

($3,900 – $300)   × ³⁄₆ = $1,800 1st Year Depreciation

($3,900 – $300)   × ²⁄₆ = $1,200 2nd Year Depreciation

($3,900 – $300)   × ¹⁄₆ = $ 600 3rd Year Depreciation
                           $3,600

Exercise 10.3

First calculate straight line rate:

$$100\% / 3 \text{ yrs} = .33 \times 2 = .66$$

Cost – Acc Dep = Book Value × Rate = Annual Depreciation

Year 1 3900 –   0 = 3900 × .66 =   2600

Year 2 3900 – 2600 = 1300 × .66 =   867

Year 3 3900 – 3467 = 433 × .66 =   133*

*The final value is adjusted down so that the final book value (cost minus accumulated depreciation) equals the salvage value that was estimated at the outset.

Exercise 10.4

$$\frac{\text{Cost}-\text{Residual Value}}{\text{Life}}$$

$$\frac{\$3,900-\$300}{10,000 \text{ hours}} = .36 \text{ per hour}$$

     2,000 hours operated this year
   ×   .36
     $720   Depreciation

Exercise 13.1

Cash Payments Journal, June, 19—

Ck. No.	Date	Payee	P/R	Explanation	Cr. Cash	Cr. Purchase Discount	Dr. Accounts Payable	Account	Dr. Amount
1	June 1	A. North	24	60-day 6% note payable	$ 303.00			{ Notes Payable	$ 300.00
2			56					{ Interest Expense	3.00
3	2 / 5	Gibson Co.	56	Overdue acct. with int.	277.75		$ 275.00	Interest Exp.	2.75
4	3 / 8	S. Stern Co.	56	Interest on mortgage for 6 mos.	6000.00			Int Exp.	6000.00
5	4 / 12	City Banks	24	2 mos. note with 10% interest	5083.33			{ Notes Payable	5000.00
6			56					{ Interest Expense	83.33
7	5 / 15	Arden Co.	56	Overdue acct. with 6% interest	361.80		360.00	Interest Expense	1.80
8	6 / 21	Tryon Mortgage Co.	56	Semi-annual 9% int on mtg	9000.00			Interest Expense	9000.00
9					$ 21,025.88		$ 635.00		$ 20,390.88
10					(11)		(21)		(X)

Exercise 13.2

Cash Receipts Journal

Date 19—	Received From	P/R	Explanation	Dr. Cash	Dr. Sales Discount	Cr. Accounts Receivable	Account	Cr. Amount
Mar. 5	L. Herbit		Overdue Acct.	$ 303		$ 300	Interest Income	$ 3
8	Bank		Interest on account	3			Interest Income	3
12	J. Crane		60-day note with interest	606			Note Receivable / Interest Income	600 / 6
13	R. Ralston		Invoice was 2%	441	$ 9	450		
15	Richards & Co.		Interest on mortgage; 1 mo.	500			Interest Income	500
18	J. Jobnson		30-day note with interest	3015			Note Receivable / Interest Income	3000 / 15
25	John Good		Overdue acct. with interest	402		400	Interest Income	2
				$ 5270	$ 9	$ 1150		$ 4129

NOTES:

GLOSSARY

accelerated depreciation
Taking highest proportion of depreciation in first year or years, often for tax advantages.

accounting cycle
Series of activities that starts with a transaction and ends with preparation of a financial statement and the closing of books.

adjusted trial balance
Balance at the end of an accounting period (usually one year) that reflects changes not recorded in day-to-day accounting.

balance sheet equation
Assets equal liabilities plus capital: $A = L + C$. Also called the accounting equation.

bank reconciliation
Verifying checking accounts and adjusting for bank charges.

bank statement
Statement sent by bank, usually monthly, showing beginning balance, all transactions occurring during the period, all bank charges incurred, and a closing balance.

bonds payable
Amounts due to bondholders of a corporation.

book value
Value of assets after depreciation has been deducted. Not necessarily the same as market value.

capital
Sum owed by a business to its owners; *owners' equity*.

cash	Total of currency, coins, money orders, checks, bank drafts, and letters of credit the firm has on hand or in bank accounts from which money can be drawn immediately.
cash payments journal	Journal for recording payments made in cash; also called a disbursements journal.
cash receipts journal	Journal for recording income received in cash; that is, not in payment of invoices that have been billed.
check register	Running record of checks written on a bank account, together with other transactions such as deposits or bank charges. See also *bank statement, bank reconciliation.*
compound entries	Entries made to record transactions that affect more than one account.
contra asset	An account that is charged against assets.
cost of goods	Amount paid for goods sold at retail or manufacturing cost of goods produced.
credit	Abbreviation *Cr.* Entry on right column.
cross referencing	Notes made in journal to show location of posting and in ledger to show location of journal entry.
current assets	1) Cash or items that will become cash in the foreseeable future because they are intended for sale. 2) Items that the business will consume within one year.
current liabilities	Claims against the business that must be paid within a year.
debit	Abbreviation *Dr.* Entry on left column.
deposit slip	A *supporting document* recording money (whether cash, check, or money order) deposited in a bank account.
discounted note	Note for which interest is deducted in advance.
double declining balance method	Method of depreciating assets.

drawee	The bank from which a check is drawn.
drawer	The person or firm drawing (making out a check).
drawing account	Ledger account showing owners' or partners' drawing of funds for personal use.
equity	Any debt a business owes, whether to itself (*owners' equity*) or to others (*liability*).
equity per share	The *owners' equity,* or capital value, of the business divided by the number of shares outstanding.
FICA	Federal Insurance Contributions Act. Taxes withheld from employees and paid by employers for "social security." Self-employed persons pay a Self-Employment Tax for the same purpose.
FIFO	First in/first out method of pricing inventory.
Form W-2	Statement of wages and withheld taxes for previous calendar year provided by employers to employees.
gross sales	Also, gross revenues. Total amount received for goods and services during the accounting period.
gross wages	An employee's compensation for the pay period before the deduction of taxes or any benefits paid by the employee. See also *net wages.*
hardware	In computer terminology, the computer itself, including its processing unit, monitor, and keyboard. See also *software.*
income summary	An account created to summarize the information from all revenue and expense accounts.
individual earnings record	Form stating all wages earned and taxes deducted for all employees during the year.
initial capital	Money and assets the owner(s) contribute to start a business.

interest rate	Percentage of principal charged per year (per annum) for "rental" of money.
inventory	Counting goods on hand for sale at end of accounting period and assigning a cost to them.
ledger	Literally, the book in which accounts are kept; used to refer to the entire set of accounts however kept (for instance, by computer).
LIFO	Last in/first out method of pricing inventory.
long-term liabilities	Equities of the business that must be paid over an interval longer than one year.
long-term note	Money borrowed by the business to be repaid after more than one year.
mortgages payable	Balance due on mortgages for business land or buildings.
net income	Amount of money left after cost of goods sold and all operating expenses have been paid.
net sales	Money left after cost of goods sold. For a manufacturing operation, direct labor may be deducted as part of cost of goods.
net wages	The amount remaining after all deductions, both for taxes and for benefits paid by the employee.
normal account balances	Balances for accounts in which increases exceed decreases.
operating margin	Net sales divided by gross sales; a guide to pricing.
operating statement	Also called "profit and loss," "P&L" or income statement. Financial report showing all income and expenses for the accounting period and calculating profit (or loss) for the period.
owners' equity	Amount left after all liabilities have been deducted from assets; portion of the assets belonging to the owners of the business; capital.
payee	Person or firm in whose name a check or other negotiable instrument is issued.

payroll deductions	Amounts withheld from an employee's pay, either for taxes or for voluntary contributions or employee-paid benefits.
payroll register	Record for each pay period, usually weekly, for entire firm, showing employee names, hours worked, straight and overtime pay, gross pay, deductions, and net pay.
petty cash	Fund set up for payment of small expenses. Part of cash on hand.
petty cash journal	Accounts showing payments made into and taken out of petty cash.
petty cash voucher	A slip or form recording recipient of funds drawn from petty cash as well as date, amount, and purpose.
plant assets	Permanent items used directly or indirectly to produce the product or service the business sells; for example, machinery, vehicles, or equipment.
posting	Entering information from journal into ledger accounts.
prepaid items	Amounts already paid for services the business has yet to receive.
purchases discount	Amount deducted from an account payable to a supplier, usually for prompt payment or quantity purchase.
purchases journal	Journal for recording purchase of items for inventory and eventual resale.
retail value	Value assigned to goods after the firm's customary markup has been added.
retained earnings	The portion of the profits that are kept and reinvested in the business rather than paid out as *dividends*.
returned goods	Merchandise returned by customers for credit or refund.

salaries	Compensation paid to supervisory and management employees who are hired at a flat yearly, monthly, and sometimes weekly compensation. See also *wages*.
sales	Money flowing into the business.
sales allowance	Price reduction given to a customer, for example, because goods are damaged.
sales discount	Discount allowed to a purchaser as opposed to a discount taken from a supplier.
sales journal	Journal for recording sales transactions.
sales returns	Refund of money to a customer.
salvage value	Residual value assigned to equipment that is fully depreciated.
software	Programs that tell a computer how to handle data, for example, word processing programs, spreadsheet programs. See also *hardware*.
spreadsheet program	Computer *software* designed to manipulate data entered into rows and columns, for example, in preparing financial projections or reports.
stockholders' equity	Value of the business divided by the number of stocks outstanding.
sum-of-years-digits method	Method of depreciating assets.
sundry account	Account assigned for expenditures that are not otherwise classified.
supplies	Materials used in conducting the daily operations of the business such as lubricants, stationery, packaging materials, as compared with raw materials or parts used in manufacturing or servicing goods.
supporting document	Written record of a transaction such as an invoice, a payroll summary, or a *petty cash voucher*.

T account	Individual ledger account.
transaction	Any occurrence in which money or goods are transferred from one party or account to another.
unadjusted trial balance	Amounts in columns 1 and 2 of the work sheet showing account totals before adjustments made at year's end.
units of production method	Method of depreciating assets.
wages	Hourly compensation paid to employees; see also *salaries*.
wages payable	Payroll due; wages and salaries owed to employees for time worked but not yet paid out.
wholesale value	The cost of an individual item held for resale; can vary over the accounting period.

INDEX